ALLY UP

ALLY UP

THE DEFINITIVE GUIDE
TO BUILDING MORE
INCLUSIVE, INNOVATIVE,
AND PRODUCTIVE TEAMS

DI CIRUOLO

NEW YORK

LONDON • NASHVILLE • MELBOURNE • VANCOUVER

ALLY UP
THE DEFINITIVE GUIDE TO BUILDING MORE INCLUSIVE, INNOVATIVE, AND PRODUCTIVE TEAMS

Published in New York, New York, by Morgan James Publishing. Morgan James is a trademark of Morgan James, LLC. www.MorganJamesPublishing.com

Morgan James BOGO™

A **FREE** ebook edition is available for you or a friend with the purchase of this print book.

_____

CLEARLY SIGN YOUR NAME ABOVE

Instructions to claim your free ebook edition:
1. Visit MorganJamesBOGO.com
2. Sign your name CLEARLY in the space above
3. Complete the form and submit a photo of this entire page
4. You or your friend can download the ebook to your preferred device

ISBN 978-1-63195-401-6 paperback
ISBN 978-1-63195-402-3 eBook
Library of Congress Control Number:
2020922531

Cover Design by:
Rachel Lopez
www.r2cdesign.com

Morgan James PUBLISHING Builds *with...* **Habitat for Humanity®** Peninsula and Greater Williamsburg

Morgan James is a proud partner of Habitat for Humanity Peninsula and Greater Williamsburg. Partners in building since 2006.

Get involved today! Visit
MorganJamesPublishing.com/giving-back

DEDICATION

For my children and all our children. May we all find the courage
to do what it takes to leave the world better than we found it.

And to my partner, Jay; thanks for believing in me.

TABLE OF CONTENTS

Foreword		ix
Preface		xiii
Introduction		xxi
Part 1: Creating a Culture That Promotes Diversity, Equity, and Inclusion		**1**
Chapter 1	Diversity Values are Devalued	5
Chapter 2	The Working-Over of Working Moms	13
Chapter 3	How Employers Can Build More Inclusive Work Cultures	21
Chapter 4	Building Communities for Social Justice	33
Part 2: Hiring with Inclusivity		**51**
Chapter 5	Attracting the Right Candidates	53
Chapter 6	Onboarding	75
Chapter 7	Building Teams and Tracking Performance	87
Part 3: Diversity, Equity, and Inclusion at Work		**107**
Chapter 8	Handling Day-to-Day Operations	113
Chapter 9	Trusting Team Members	125
Chapter 10	Leading by Example	137
	Conclusion	153
	Acknowledgments	157
	Social Justice Resources:	159
	About the Author	167

FOREWORD

As a radio show host for most of my life, I could hide behind the mic and be anything I'd like. Nobody would ever know if I was wearing fleece pajamas with little Christmas trees all over them or wiping off a milk mustache from my bowl of Cheerios. I could be whoever I wanted to be, from a shock jock to someone who knew a lot about, say, New Zealand frigate birds.

While a lot of people choose a persona when they enter radio, I chose to just be myself from the get-go. Long before authenticity became the latest buzzword, I'd welcome guests by being transparent, open, and vulnerable. If I felt self-conscious about something, I'd say it. If I didn't know an answer, I'd say so.

Little did I know that being open and honest with the world would impact millions of listeners—and, in one very special instance, Di Ciruolo.

In 2005, I spent several shows opening up about being betrayed by my mother's and family's painful dysfunctional issues. I was heartbroken and chose to share these stories with my listeners. I even talked about how I was seeking therapy to end the cycle of dysfunction. I shared how my therapist encouraged me and changed my perspective about my family. I talked about how I learned that the dysfunction wasn't my fault, or anybody's fault, and I encouraged listeners to seek therapy for anything they were carrying around with them, especially with handling family issues. My goal was to show my audience that goodness can come out of some of the worst situations.

Later on in one of the shows, my producers told me that Tyler Perry—*the* Tyler Perry—was calling in to share a story about him being homeless and navigating toxic and unloving relationships. He told me, "People aren't lying awake at night thinking about how they hurt you and what they did. Only you're doing that. Stop letting people live rent-free in your head. When you let go of the anger, you can get better. You can be better. You can have a future."

These were some of the most authentic, raw conversations we've had on *The Bert Show*. I knew in the moment that our conversation would help people, but I had no idea who. More than a decade later, I learned that Di Ciruolo was listening that day. I learned that my conversation with Tyler Perry motivated her to start therapy and that Tyler Perry's words of wisdom changed everything for her.

"Suddenly there were people like me who came from where I came from and made it out," Di wrote to me, recently. "Suddenly there were people who I could aspire to be who survived what I'd survived. It changed everything for me. And I will never forget it, nor stop being grateful to two people who shared their stories honestly and authentically not knowing what the ripples would bring back."

While we don't know how far those ripples will extend, we do know they have brought us *Ally Up*, a book about diversity, equity, and inclusion in the workplace. At its heart, *Ally Up* is a book about authenticity, openness, and transparency in the workforce. It's a story about speaking out and being honest with each other to help lift each other up to a place where we can all thrive in welcoming and accepting workplaces where everyone can succeed. It's about the power we have when we take off our masks and share our vulnerabilities as humans instead of whatever labels people have assigned to us. It's about finding the empathy to truly connect with and stand up for others. It's about becoming an ally.

We can be allies.

To do so, however, we must first commit to standing up for others and speaking out, even when it's uncomfortable for us to do so. It's about being open, honest, and transparent in each of our relationships with others. It's about working together to achieve a common goal of acceptance and equality so everyone can thrive together in a truly collaborative and inclusive workplace.

I applaud Di for doing the hard work it took for her to leave her past in the past and build resources to help make the world a better place for everyone. While the specifics of her journey might be different from yours, I hope her willingness to lead uncomfortable conversations to make the world a better place will inspire you like it does me. And I hope that her experience and wisdom have the same impact on you that my conversation with Tyler Perry had on her—to inspire you to take action and, in this case, do the hard work it will take to become an ally for a more diverse, equal, and inclusive workforce.

Bert Weiss
The Bert Show

PREFACE

Welcome to my allyship.

I came to the field of diversity, equity, and inclusion because I was angry.

My entire childhood was spent in the foster care system in Massachusetts, just north of Boston. I'd been removed when I was three—when folks noticed I was coming into preschool filthy, malnourished, and with lice and ringworm. I was smart; I'd tried to hide it. I'd gone back with my birth family a few times but was always removed again. I was finally removed the final time when one of my mother's boyfriends started sexually abusing me. That was it for the State of Massachusetts.

If you've been part of the foster care system, you know it went from bad to worse. After bouncing around from hellscape to hellscape, full of more abuse than I have the heart to recall here, I landed in a permanent care situation at age seven. Unfortunately, this was with a foster mother who was seriously damaged and took me on as a domestic servant. In public, I was a member of her family she'd saved from abuse and rape—and she would tell anyone who would listen all about it directly in front of me. Othering me. Dehumanizing me. I'd hear how lucky I was, how grateful I should be. But at home, everything was different. I wasn't allowed to eat the same food. All of my clothes were donations from other kids at school or from family. I was beaten constantly, often nearly to death. I couldn't do homework or have friends, and everyone knew. Even adults knew what was happening to me and accepted it on my behalf. "Be grateful," I'd hear. "It could be worse for you."

When I aged out of foster care, I was homeless. My foster mother had told everyone she'd adopted me, but in fact, that hadn't been true at all. The second she stopped receiving money from the State of Massachusetts, suddenly it was, "You've never tried hard enough to be a member of this family." In my desperation to survive, I moved from Boston to Atlanta, where the rent was cheaper, people accepted me, and everything just felt easier. Against the statistics for kids like me going through what I went through, I got better. I made friends who'd survived their own childhoods. Atlanta is full of good people who helped raise me. I worked hard to have extra money for therapy. I put myself through college at Georgia State University. I did well. I headed up committees and served on different student boards. I completed an internship as a child advocate and was the only nonlaw student to have done so in the program's history at the time. Now it's open to everyone.

I got used to having to earn my way, to being the first like me, and I didn't mind because it meant that I was good. That's what I told myself. This will all be worth it. I had friends who went to "better" schools—Duke, Emory, UNC—but I was finishing my degree in anthropology,[1] race, and gender studies, and doing my senior project on how race (a social construct) impacted tuberculosis and drug resistance in the Atlanta area. All the while, I was watching my Ivy League friends run interview prep together. They had access to better-paying jobs—and likely better

---

1   Everyone told me anthropology was useless, but it's basically a precursor to diversity, equity, and inclusion, or DEI, work—so how about now?

futures—because recruiters from elite, well-known companies came to their campuses to recruit them. When I called, emailed, and networked with people to try to get an interview for one of those coveted positions, I was told, "Sorry, we don't take unsolicited resumes." Over and over again. When it came right down to it, because I didn't go to an Ivy League school, I wasn't worthy of the time it took to interview me. I didn't lack hustle; I lacked privilege. Hiring has always been a game of exclusion.

And Therein Lies the Question: Who Is This System Working For?

That question drove me to what I do today; I help teams and individuals with diversity, equity, and inclusion in professional settings. Or rather, I teach people how allyship builds more-diverse, equitable, and inclusive businesses.

Why should people care about being allies? If the current system works for you, you might not see a need for allies in the workplace. You might think the workplace is a meritocracy, and because you worked hard to get where you are, you might think anyone can follow the same path to success. Maybe they just don't work hard enough. You might also be tired of hearing people say that people who look like you are to blame for the inequalities all around us. Allyship isn't about blame; it's about action. And I am happy to show you why allyship is crucial for you too.

Let's Take a Walk

What if I could help you visualize how inequality works in the workplace? In a book, it's hard. In person, it's a lot easier with a diversity walk. My favorite way to demonstrate inequality is with a diversity walk. If you can't do a diversity walk, you can check out the video in the footnotes below.

In this video,[2] you'll see a group of racially diverse college students of all genders lining up next to each other for a race. A prompter explains the rules of the race. The winner of the race will get a $100 bill. Everyone is excitedly chatting and warming up.

Before the race begins, the prompter explains the rules:

"I'm going to make a couple statements; if those statements apply to you, I want you to take two steps forward. If those statements don't apply to you, I want you to stay right where you're at."

"Take two steps forward," the prompter instructs, "if both of your parents are still married."

Many participants step forward.

He gives them more instructions. "Take two steps forward if you never wondered where your next meal was going to come from."

Some participants step forward. This continues throughout the exercise, with the prompter providing more and more criteria.

A more obvious division between the students develops.

"Take two steps forward if you had access to a free tutor growing up."

"Take two steps forward if you never had to help Mom or Dad with the bills."

"Take two steps forward if—it wasn't because of your athletic ability—you don't have to pay for college."

By now, something visually obvious is happening. The people in front have been taking giant steps forward, thrilled with their luck, never turning around to see what is happening to anyone behind them. Many assume everyone is taking the same steps forward as them as they look around at their friends advancing also. Meanwhile, a smaller and more racially diverse segment of students is still standing on the original

---

2   "Privilege/Class/Social Inequalities Explained in a $100 Race," Peter D, October 14, 2017, YouTube video, 4:12, https://www.youtube.com/watch?v=4K5fbQ1-zps.

starting line, realizing by about the second prompt what's happening. A few even look defeated—what's the point of racing at all with this much of a disadvantage? The prompter has the students in front turn around.

This is life, he tells them. Simply because of their life circumstances, the students at the front have a massive head start to the race. Therefore, they have a much-increased chance of winning the $100.

He tells the people who are closer to the finish line that they're not closer because of anything they've done. The folks in the back aren't there because of anything they've done. And yet the folks in the front have an enormous advantage.

"If this was a fair race...I guarantee you some of these Black dudes would smoke all of you."

"Does that mean these people back here can't race?" he asks, pointing to the original starting line.

"There's no excuse. They still gotta run that race. You still gotta run your race...That is a picture of life, ladies and gentlemen."

"On your mark, get set, go!" Everyone runs as fast as they can to the same finish line, and you never see the outcome.

The Race We're All Running

While the "race" in the video was set up to demonstrate the point, it reflects exactly what is happening in the world with respect to inequality.

Yes, it's true that those students, regardless of their head start, or lack thereof, had to run the same race. That is technically true.

But the crucial point is to visually demonstrate how large a gap there was between the kids who were disadvantaged and the kids who had no idea such disadvantages even existed.

The finish line might have been the same, but the starting line was much, much different.

And that is what actually exists in life and in the workforce. When I write and talk about allyship, I'm not asking you to examine your morals. I am asking you to examine your privilege. How many leaps forward would you have taken if you were in that video? Where would your starting line be? Where would your coworkers' starting lines be? You're reading my book: where would I be?

Allyship is not about changing the finish line; it's about teaching people at the front of the race with an enormous head start to own the privilege, lean in, and work hard to make the race more equitable.

Obviously, to continue the metaphor, it would be better to change the rules of the race so everyone starts at the same point, and only the best advance. A true meritocracy. But that requires systemic change, and as yet, we aren't there. I don't know that we will ever be there. But we won't get there without allyship.

Your Diversity Story

I believe everyone has a diversity story, and everyone has a role to play in the changes we so desperately need to make. We know that people of color often put themselves at great risk by bringing up biases they see in the workplace. This is especially true with Black women+.[3] And when they do, they're often accused of playing "the race card" or "making it about race."

This happens at all levels. When Rosalind Brewer, then Sam's Club CEO[4] and a Black woman, advocated for working only with vendors that have a commitment to diversity on their teams, she was called a racist.[5]

---

3   Whenever a "+" follows the word *women* or *LGBTQ*, it is intended to include more groups of people who share an identity beyond what is named. So, *women+* means not only women, but trans women as well. Trans women are women, of course, but this is the notation that lets you know I specifically intended to include them.

4   Roz Brewer is now CEO of Walgreens as of 2021.

5   Hayley Peterson, "People Are Calling Sam's Club CEO 'Racist' after She Gave an Interview about Diversity," *Business Insider*, December 14, 2015,

And it's everywhere. When I see a statistic that 85% of corporate executives and board members are white men,[6] I know it's because white managers promote people who look like them. In many cases, at least, they're not intentionally excluding people who don't look like them. But that doesn't change the fact that only white men can get away with that. That's the point. It's not enough for those of us who have made it against the odds to speak for others. It's not enough to keep your head down and trudge silently through discrimination and racist jokes. It's not enough for everyone to compete for that one seat at the table that's reserved for someone other than a white man. If we don't teach people how to be allies, progress stagnates for everyone. There will *always* be only one seat—if any—if we don't all become allies. We need to give allies the knowledge and the vocabulary to make them effective at speaking out when they see inequality.

I don't believe you can be an expert in this field. I've been in this fight for all of my adult life, and I can assure you there are people and issues I'm not an expert on. I believe having a deep understanding of allyship and inclusion means you've committed to being a lifelong learner and being passionately okay with being wrong some of the time. I'm here because the house is on fire. I'm not waiting for someone else's permission to pick up a bucket, and you shouldn't either.

Look at me, and you'll see a light-skinned woman. Listen to me, and you'll hear me talk about my partner—I'm happily married to a cisgendered man, and we have two incredible kids. Judge me, and you'll wonder, as so many have, how can you be an authority on diversity with any authenticity? But consider, it is not the job of people of

---

https://www.businessinsider.com/sams-club-ceo-accused-of-racism-after-cnn-interview-2015-12.

6 Stefanie K. Johnson and David R. Hekman, "Women and Minorities Are Penalized for Promoting Diversity," *Harvard Business Review*, March 23, 2016, https://hbr.org/2016/03/women-and-minorities-are-penalized-for-promoting-diversity.

xx | ALLY UP

underrepresented backgrounds to teach you how to be an ally. People of color and underrepresented groups don't benefit from these systems. When we place the unfair burden of arguing for equality in the workplace on anyone of a diverse background, we are causing them harm by asking them for a business case for why they deserve to be there and why they deserve to be treated as equals. We need allies to be educated and prepared to move the needle in the workforce.

Now, let's get to work. It's time to ally up.

INTRODUCTION

"The future of our culture—our country—depends not so much on what Black people do as it does on what white people do. Now, this is a hard lesson for some of us. That the choice as to whether or not we will rid the country of racism is a choice that White America has to make."

—Ella Baker, activist, 1968

When I talk to white folks, I often hear how much they want to be allies. How they don't see color. Look, first lesson: remove that sentence from your entire lexicon. Trust me, we'll get to that. When I discuss allyship with disenfranchised communities about allies, I often get a range of negative emotions from a full-on eye roll to outright anger. From our position, a person who calls themself an ally but has no record within the community of acting as one (or has the receipts, as we say), is like a guy who calls himself a feminist to get laid. Yuck, right? That's the same.

Similarly, when white folks say "allies," it continues the idea that unequal systems—racism, misogyny, homophobia, transphobia, etc.— are the problems of those marginalized groups and we are "allying" with them because we are so decent and woke, rather than the truth that these systems are propped up and furthered by people who benefit from them, not those that they oppress. That's a pretty big difference that isn't just semantics. For my purposes, when I talk about how to "ally up!" I'm using "ally" as a verb. I want to teach folks how to be effective allies/ advocates by promoting allyship in the workplace and life, and I'm using more approachable language to that end.

Why Tech?

When I'm interviewed, I'm often asked, "Why do you work in tech?" or, "Why is this tech's problem?" I'm an older millennial. Not "older" in general, but on the upper end for millennials. I remember a time before computers were in every home. Before the Internet. For those of us in our thirties who came of age with modern-day tech, who started using Facebook when Zuck et al. created it, we've always looked to tech as the future's frontier. A place where everything is possible if you can imagine it (and have a VC to back you, amiright?). Tech is the future, and rightly or wrongly, it's where we can live in a world that didn't exist yesterday. We all want these oppressive structures to be a thing of the past, to have these problems "solved." For me, if tech can't solve this problem, then I'm not sure a solution exists. Tech has to work to get this right, or there isn't any hope for other industries with less time, less money, and less creative problem-solving or less innovative imagination. Maybe that's unfair, but I don't believe it is. We have presented tech with unimaginable human problems, and it just smiles and churns out the most efficient and creative solutions. Then it fights its competitors off and rises from the ashes again and again until it has the best possible solution. Those who can't adapt, die. Maybe that's a little romantic, but Elon Musk[7] got folks out of a mineshaft live on Twitter. Don't tell me we can't improve on this. We have some of the best minds in the world: We have to work on this. We have to prioritize it. We have to be willing to shrug off the institutions of what we know and question why we know it. Who is being included? Who is being excluded? Whose perspectives are not here, and why aren't they? How does that impact what we think we know? Tech can handle it. It has to.

In this book, I will be using *a lot* of research, interviews, and voices by others to support my claims; that's on purpose. Could I talk from the preface to the conclusion nonstop? Yes. If my report cards are anything to go by, I definitely could.[8] Do I think that's a thorough representation or understanding of the scholarship needed to be an effective ally? Not at all.

My experience leads me to believe that a large subset of the Caucasian population wants to be effective allies. They want to do right by their businesses, their friends, and their communities, but we, as a society, don't teach the vocabulary. Why would we? A lot of white folks I talk to will recount a situation they saw and knew was wrong, but they weren't sure if it was appropriate to say something. How do you say something? What do you say? Will the victim of that situation be happy you stepped in or will they feel angry? I'm writing this book for you. A lot of people of color will recount a situation where they were victimized at work

---

7 Radhika Viswanathan, "Elon Musk's Plan to Bring a Mini-Submarine to Rescue the Thai Boys," *Vox*, July 11, 2018, https://www.vox.com/2018/7/10/17553820/elon-musk-thai-cave-rescue-submarine. Latest alleged Twitter scandals notwithstanding.

8 Yes, my report cards all noted that I talked nonstop. My college internship exit interview said the same. I've worked hard to listen more than I speak, but I'm a work in progress.

and no one did anything in the moment, but their white friends later apologized and let them know they knew it was wrong. I'm here for you too. We need a baseline of information on how to talk to each other about diversity so we can be inclusive as a community.

For people of color, I'm not fighting for you specifically. I'm fighting against the system. I love you, and so many of you have made me what I am today, but these racist systems aren't yours. This fight is mine because I benefit from some privileges and because I have also suffered oppression and dehumanization. I have been a victim of this system since before I can remember, all the while being reminded how grateful I should be and to be nice about things I ask for. I have had limitations and stipulations put on my life and what I was allowed to dream for. I have worked every single day to get to where I believe I deserve to be in spite of folks laughing in my face, moving the goalposts away, and telling me they "support" me or are "inspired" by how far I've come. I've even had people draw the conclusion that if I "can do it, then no one has an excuse." But that isn't true. Because "If I can do it, anyone can" is an illusory narrative that disproportionately punishes people who didn't make it out, and lets people benefiting from the status quo sleep better at night knowing that the "pull yourself up by your bootstraps" narrative is real, and people in poverty just aren't working hard enough to get out. I will never allow anyone to use my story to support that narrative. I carry a tremendous amount of survivor's guilt for those kids. I'm not standing up to take over or to save anyone. I'm here to teach allyship and help force change. That's a tightrope to walk, and I'll mess up, but I'm here, and I'm doing the work.

"While this movement may be started by Black people and may be carried on the backs of Black people, it's going to cross the finish line on the backs of white people, and it's important that we educate them, that we challenge them to get involved, to learn what's going

on, because the only way we really see it getting all the way through fruition is going to be if we get white people to bring this to a majority rule."

—Malcolm Jenkins

Everyone Is Biased

First of all, let's talk about biases. You're biased, I'm biased, everyone is biased. I'm not calling you a racist or saying this is your fault. It just so happens that this is the way the human brain works. Biases are basically shortcuts that our human brains make. A brain is exposed to 11 million bits of information on a moment-to-moment basis and is able to process about 40 bits at a time. The difference is covered by the unconscious in the form of guesses based on previously held information biases. Your biases exist to help your brain keep you safe, physically and socially. Our biases in their natural state benefit our own groups, the groups we belong to, and denigrate the groups we don't belong to. Blatant discrimination is not over by any means, but discrimination these days tends to be subtler. It's hard to hold on to. It's hard to prove. Worst of all, the onus is on the victim of the situation to prove that they were discriminated against. The perpetrator can basically dig out any old excuse and is almost always given the benefit of the doubt. It's unfortunate, but that's where we are.

When I'm called up to consult or speak, the request I hear the most is, "I don't want to hear the 'woo-woo' side of diversity. I want the business case for diversity."[9] If you're white, you're thinking: *Exactly.* If you're a person of color, you're thinking: *What?! What's the business case for white people belonging anywhere over anyone else?!* I know. That's another one of those perspective shifts that contextualizes how we think about the status quo. Asking about the business case for diversity seems like an innocent request, but you should think about the place it comes

---

9 Everyone seems to use the expression "woo-woo." I have no idea why.

from and how other people might hear it. For this book, to answer that question, I'll dig into the science—and the studies, you'll see, are innumerable.

Biases at Work

To illustrate how implicit biases can affect the workplace, look no further than the 2003 study by Marianne Bertrand and Sendhil Mullainathan[10] asking, "Are Emily and Greg more employable than Lakisha and Jamal?" In the study, the researchers sent identical resumes applying for open positions to a real hiring company with one key difference—the owner of the resume would have either a traditionally white name or a traditionally Black name. You may be surprised to find out that the traditionally white names received 50% more callbacks for interviews. The amount of discrimination was tested across occupations and industries and was found to be identical. Federal employers who tout being equal opportunity employers in their job description were found to discriminate just as much as other employers. There was also little evidence in the results of the study that employers were able to infer something other than race, such as social class, from the names.

Implicit Bias

Implicit bias, as noted above, exists in everyone, and if we want to move forward, we need to discover and accept where we are. If you want to test your implicit biases, and you should, I recommend Project Implicit[11] by Harvard University. You can test your biases against race,

---

10   Marianne Bertrand and Sendhil Mullainathan, "Are Emily and Greg More Employable than Lakisha and Jamal? A Field Experiment on Labor Market Discrimination," NBER Working Paper No. w9873, National Bureau of Economic Research, Cambridge, MA, (July 2003), https://doi.org/10.2139/ssrn.422902.

11   Project Implicit, "Take a Test," Harvard.edu (Project Implicit, 2011), https://implicit.harvard.edu/implicit/takeatest.html.

gender, sexual orientation, the differently abled, and many more. Project Implicit explains how these implicit association tests (IATs) can help determine how closely seemingly disparate concepts are connected in your mind. Once you know where your biases lead you, you can do the work to correct them. Again, you should not be ashamed of your results because we all hold biases (remember, our brains do this automatically). You should only be ashamed if you can't be bothered to do the work to change them, and if you're reading this book, I know you're here and ready to do the work. Furthermore, you can take these tests before and after reading this book to see how much progress you've made. Science suggests with practice and understanding, you will likely improve. So let's define our terms.

Terms and Definitions

Stereotypes, Prejudice, and Discrimination

A **stereotype** is a belief that we hold about the attributes or characteristics that a person from another group might have. They are widely known throughout a culture, which makes them insidious due to their automatic evocation, even if you don't believe in or agree with them.

Prejudice is a negative attitude we have about those in other groups that is based off of stereotypes and sweeping generalizations. Historically, these ideas can present in dehumanization propaganda and have been seen across time. Examples include slavery, the Holocaust, the AIDS epidemic, and the U.S. border crisis. Prejudice can also present in more subtle ways:

- *Ambivalent prejudice* is when a person thinks about an out-group and experiences a negative feeling without attributing it to one specific experience or person.

- *Aversive prejudice* (racism) is when negative feelings about an out-group cause one to avoid being around those types of people. Self-segregating is a form of aversive prejudice.

"Prejudice is an emotional commitment to ignorance."
    —**Nathan Rutstein**

Discrimination is an action or a behavior one takes based on prejudices and stereotypes. It is also a choice. People can have prejudices they don't act on. Discrimination is treating people differently based on the out-group they belong to. For example, if a company finds that Hispanic, Asian, Black, and white people apply to its jobs at the same rate, but only one race is represented in its workforce, it likely has a discrimination problem.

One of the effects of stereotyping is a biased interpretation of information that is unclear or ambiguous.

As far back as the '80s, we've known this. In 1983, researchers John Darley and Paget Gross[12] showed a group of participants a video of a little girl answering age-appropriate, school-based questions in a classroom setting. Some questions she got right, some she got wrong. The difference was the researchers included a pre-video, which showed the little girl walking in either an affluent neighborhood or a lower-class neighborhood. Darley and Gross asked the participants, "How smart is this little girl?" to see how her neighborhood affected the answer. They found that if they showed the video where she was from an affluent community, she was perceived to have a higher ability. If she was from a lower-class neighborhood, she was perceived to have a lower ability. How do we account for this? According to the research, people were

---

12　John M. Darley and Paget H. Gross, "A Hypothesis-Confirming Bias in Labeling Effects," *Journal of Personality and Social Psychology* 44, no. 1 (1983): 20–33, https://doi.org/10.1037/0022-3514.44.1.20.

misremembering her performance, which was the same both times. They also changed their internal criteria for the questions, implying that the questions she answered correctly were worth more than the questions she answered incorrectly.

So now that we know stereotypes lead people to draw erroneous conclusions based on ambiguous events, how might this play out in a work setting?

In-Groups and Out-Groups

Have you ever had the experience where you learn something about someone that makes you like them right away? Yes, right? Common ground connects us. Maybe this person likes the same sports team as you; maybe they went to the same school as you; maybe they grew up in the same city as you—whatever you share, social scientists call this an "in-group," and it will bias you toward them and bias you against those who don't share your in-groups. I still like emo and love hip-hop (mind your own business), and when I meet people who share my taste in music, I feel like I know them in my heart. If you don't like country music, you may draw the conclusion you won't like people who like country music. It can be that simple and meaningless.

The reason we like people like us is we think we are good people. If we are on a team, and the people at work like us, why wouldn't more people "like us" be right for the company?

The challenge is that having more people "like us" creates bad solutions to problems, especially the more complex ones. When everyone on the team looks the same and thinks the same, we unknowingly create echo chambers. Diversity is a powerful competitive advantage that leads to more innovative solutions. Furthermore, people tend to share and challenge their assumptions more when in a diverse group than they do in a group where everyone is the same.

As it turns out, group stereotypes bias our evaluations of individuals, especially when the stereotype matches the judgment. In a 2017 study, Rattan, Steele, and Ambady[13] considered how Asian women were judged for a job placement as a computer technician. If the hiring managers focused more on the fact she was Asian than she was a woman, then she was more likely to be given a better offer and starting pay. If they focused more on the fact that she identified as a woman, she was considered less qualified and offered less compensation.

Can small and ultimately meaningless in-groups still produce bias? Yes. It *does not matter how insignificant the difference is*, according to the minimal group paradigm: just the fact that the group exists creates in-groups and out-groups. There are even in-groups and out-groups that exist within fandoms of the same television or book series. This isn't because we're inherently closed-minded; it's just our human brains trying to protect us by finding comfortable nesting grounds. How many programmers do you know willing to go to war on the spaces vs. tabs debate? Oh, everyone? That's why.

Priming for Stereotypes

When we talk about priming, what we mean is that the participant (or candidate) has been reminded about a stereotype and their relationship to this stereotype based on their identity. This can be as subtle as asking a participant to fill out their race and gender on an application for employment. Stereotypes are insidious, and they affect memory. They can even impact our own memories about things that we experienced firsthand.

---

13   Aneeta Rattan, Jennifer Steele, and Nalini Ambady, "Identical Applicant but Different Outcomes: The Impact of Gender versus Race Salience in Hiring," *Group Processes & Intergroup Relations* 22, no. 1 (August 17, 2017): 80–97, https://doi.org/10.1177/1368430217722035.

A French study in 2007 by Chatard, Guimond, and Selimbegovic[14] tested the memory of teenage students and their standardized testing grades from two years prior. Before being asked about their scores, the researchers "primed" the students by reminding them how stereotypes suggest girls are bad at math. When researchers asked their math scores from two years earlier, female students misremembered their scores as being lower, and male students misremembered their scores as being higher. In order to correct for the idea that maybe the male students were just overconfident, they also tested the students' memory of their art scores. The female students misremembered their art scores as being higher than they were, and the male students remembered their art scores being lower.

Stereotypes about our in-groups can guide how we feel about ourselves as individuals.

Stereotype Threat

In 1992, Claude Steele and Joshua Aronson created the term "stereotype threat."[15] Basically, it's when you find yourself in a situation where you're scared of conforming to the negative stereotype associated with your in-group. Sometimes we see situations where women+, people of color, and the LGBTQ+ community feel like if they fail, they won't be judged as individuals but as members of a certain group. For example, if I fail in a new situation as a woman, I worry that I'll make it harder for all women who come after me. If I fail at something while being a Hispanic person, will my failures be felt by all of my in-group who

---

14 Armand Chatard, Serge Guimond, and Leila Selimbegovic, "'How Good Are You in Math?' The Effect of Gender Stereotypes on Students' Recollection of Their School Marks," *Journal of Experimental Social Psychology* 43, no. 6 (November 2007): 1017–24, https://doi.org/10.1016/j.jesp.2006.10.024.

15 Claude M. Steele and Joshua Aronson, "Stereotype Threat and the Intellectual Test Performance of African Americans," *Journal of Personality and Social Psychology* 69, no. 5 (1995): 797–811, https://doi.org/10.1037//0022-3514.69.5.797.

want to come up after me? Have I destroyed their chances? Guilt. Panic. Shame spiral. This is stereotype threat.

To include a quote from my future friend, Neil deGrasse Tyson:[16] "In the perception of society, my athletic talents are genetic; I am a likely mugger/rapist; my academic failures are expected; and my academic successes are attributed to others. To spend most of my life fighting these attitudes levies an emotional tax that is a form of intellectual emasculation."

Steele and Aronson also coauthored a 1995 study on race and intelligence,[17] testing Black and white students' ability to answer SAT questions. In one condition, they gave no additional instructions, and both Black and white students performed the same. In the second condition, the researchers "primed" the students by saying the study was to test "general intelligence." In that situation, Black students underperformed by half. Group differences were found *only* when students were "primed" with the stereotype that white students were smarter.

In 1999, Jeff Stone at the University of Arizona[18] led a similar study of race and athletic performance. The researchers set up an "athletic aptitude test" in the form of a mini-golf competition. In condition one, they gave students no additional instructions, and the students performed the same. In condition two, they told students it was a test of "sports intelligence," and white students performed better than Black students. In the third condition, researchers told

---

16 Yes, I said "future friend." We haven't met, but someday we will, and I will be delighted. I'm available for a coffee seven days a week, Dr. Neil.

17 Claude M. Steele and Joshua Aronson, "Stereotype Threat and the Intellectual Test Performance of African Americans," *Journal of Personality and Social Psychology* 69, no. 5 (1995): 797–811, https://doi.org/10.1037//0022-3514.69.5.797.

18 Jeff Stone et al., "Stereotype Threat Effects on Black and White Athletic Performance," *Journal of Personality and Social Psychology* 77, no. 6 (1999): 1213–27, https://doi.org/10.1037/0022-3514.77.6.1213.

the students that the test was measuring "natural ability," and Black students outperformed white students. Nothing else about the conditions themselves changed throughout the study—only the information they primed the students with.

The American Psychological Association has more than 400 studies measuring how stereotype threat and being reminded of negative stereotypes negatively impacts performance.

For stereotype threat to be in play, four conditions need to exist. First, the person must be aware of the negative stereotype about the group they belong to. Second, the test must be diagnostic of the ability; that is, the test must accurately measure ability. Third, the task needs to be difficult, and finally, the person must identify strongly with the stereotyped group and care about the task at hand.

Each of these conditions negatively affect professional outcomes for members of minority groups all the time. For example, if a woman is taking a coding test to join an engineering team at a company with other women in similar roles, she doesn't feel singled out, and she does well. On the other hand, if she is taking a coding test among men as the one and only woman, she will likely do worse. If she does poorly in conditions where an organization has fewer women+ represented, what have you accurately measured?

Combating Stereotype Threat

In 2009, David Marx, Sei Jin Ko, and Ray Friedman[19] tested what they called "The Obama Effect." Researchers gave Black and white students a verbal test multiple times. When President Obama was experiencing success (for example, right after his election), Black

19   David Marx, Sei Jin Ko, and Ray Friedman, "The 'Obama Effect': How a Salient Role Model Reduces Race-Based Performance Differences," *Journal of Experimental Social Psychology* 45 (2009): 953–56, https://doi.org/10.1016/j.jesp.2009.03.012.

students did measurably better. This didn't affect white students, so it wasn't that the student body got better at test-taking. The researchers were able to repeat this effect each time, and the achievement gap was lowest when President Obama was a clear role model and his popularity was greatest.

You can't be what you can't see. You've likely heard this before—if there aren't role models or leaders who look like us at the top of our profession, we will get the subtle (and sometimes overt) message that we don't belong there. It's why the photograph by Pete Souza of five-year-old Jacob Philadelphia touching President Barack Obama's hair in 2009[20] was so moving. He said: "I want to know if your hair is like mine," and President Obama reportedly leaned down and said, "Touch it, dude!" Role models matter. Representation matters.

In 2003, Catherine Good, Joshua Aronson, and Michael Inzlicht[21] set out to test why gender and race gaps continue to exist in standardized testing. They hypothesized that stereotype threat and stereotypes denigrate the math skills of girls and the intelligence of Black and Hispanic students. The researchers paired 7th graders with college-aged mentors, who taught the students that the mind was a muscle, and they could increase intelligence with work. Before this "mindset change," boys did better at math than girls; after the "mindset change," the gender gap disappeared. What happened? Did the girls magically get smarter? No. They were supported and mentored and improved with work. They found similar results when observing gaps attributed to race and GPA scores.

---

20 Jacob Philadelphia, "The Story of the Boy Who Touched Obama's Hair (HBO)," VICE News, June 16, 2017, YouTube video, 2:09, https://www.youtube.com/watch?v=-x_2zyGcVZ8.

21 Catherine Good, Joshua Aronson, and Michael Inzlicht, "Improving Adolescents' Standardized Test Performance: An Intervention to Reduce the Effects of Stereotype Threat," *Journal of Applied Developmental Psychology* 24, no. 6 (December 2003): 645–62, https://doi.org/10.1016/j.appdev.2003.09.002.

A study sought to challenge the achievement gap[22] between white and Hispanic students with positive affirmations reminding students about their worth and their values before each test. They found this not only reduced the achievement gap markedly but also that these results were still having a positive effect two years later.

These studies and the 400-plus others demonstrate the repeatable and observable impact that mentorship and awareness have on outcomes in schools and in the workforce.

The Ideologies of Diversity

Social science has two ideologies when it comes to approaches in diversity: multiculturalism and color-blindness.

Multiculturalism

The multiculturalism approach highlights group membership as a strength and something to be valued—which is the way it's taught to minorities in groups and families. All-inclusive multiculturalism (AIM) recognizes group differences and the roles that minorities and nonminorities play. It allows for everyone to contribute to diversity, have a diversity story, and be wholly themselves and celebrated for who they are.

A 2008 study by Flannery G. Stevens, Victoria C. Plaut, and Jeffrey Sanchez-Burks[23] found that AIM helps develop positive and productive workplace change with the formation of social capital and positive

---

22 Barbara Schneider, Sylvia Martinez, and Ann Ownes, "Barriers to Educational Opportunities for Hispanics in the United States," in *Hispanics and the Future of America* (Washington DC: National Academies Press (US), 2006), https://www. ncbi.nlm.nih.gov/books/NBK19909/.

23 Flannery G. Stevens, Victoria C. Plaut, and Jeffrey Sanchez-Burks, "Unlocking the Benefits of Diversity: All-Inclusive Multiculturalism and Positive Organizational Change," *The Journal of Applied Behavioral Science* 44, no. 1 (March 2008): 116–33, https://doi.org/10.1177/0021886308314460.

relationships allowing people to feel safe and supported to be their whole selves and bring their good ideas to work with them.

Color-Blindness

I promised you we'd get to it, and here we are—let's talk about the expression "I don't see color." Color-blindness is intended to be egalitarian and meritocratic. We think that saying, "I don't see color" is equal to proving one's not a racist. In fact, the opposite is true. While it is often well-meaning and well-intentioned, color-blindness is empirically the wrong approach to diversity. According to a study by Plaut, Thomas, and Goren in 2009,[24] color-blindness "predicts increased bias and thus contributes to a negative diversity climate." On the other hand, departments that embraced multiculturalism were thought to be less biased, and more minority colleagues were interested in working in those departments.

Researchers from the University of Colorado at Boulder and the University of Chicago found that contrary to the implicit assumption that color-blindness leads to prejudice reduction, in fact, it leads to more explicit and implicit prejudice when compared to multiculturalism.[25]

Similarly, a study by Evan P. Apfelbaum, Michael I. Norton, and Samuel R. Sommers[26] found that color-blindness, while pervasive as a management style to diversity in businesses and institutions, is actually less friendly and less effective than we've been led to believe.

---

24 Victoria C. Plaut, Kecia M. Thomas, and Matt J. Goren, "Is Multiculturalism or Color Blindness Better for Minorities?," *Psychological Science* 20, no. 4 (April 2009): 444–46, https://doi.org/10.1111/j.1467-9280.2009.02318.x.

25 Correll, Joshua, Bernadette Park, and J. Allegra Smith. "Colorblind and Multicultural Prejudice Reduction Strategies in High-Conflict Situations." Group Processes & Intergroup Relations 11, no. 4 (October 2008): 471–91. https://doi.org/10.1177/1368430208095401.

26 Evan P. Apfelbaum, Michael I. Norton, and Samuel R. Sommers, "Racial Color Blindness," *Current Directions in Psychological Science* 21, no. 3 (May 30, 2012): 205–9, https://doi.org/10.1177/0963721411434980.

Underrepresented Groups (URGs)

This term is what we use for groups that are underrepresented, which is the term for the rate at which an affinity group exists in life locally isn't the same as in the workforce. For tech and STEM fields more widely, that's women+, people of color, LGBTQ+, and others. For short, we say URG. If we mean only people of color, we say POC: people of color, or BIPOC: Black, Indigenous, and people of color.

Intersectionality

The term *intersectionality* was first used by Professor Kimberlé Crenshaw[27] of Columbia Law School 30 years ago and has come a long way since then. She had intended to describe that members of the Black community would be impacted by laws differently based on other parts of their identity, such as gender. For our purposes, I want to address its current meaning, which is to describe how people within an affinity group might be impacted differently by other contributing pieces of their identity as it relates to social and workplace laws and policies. For example, even within the LGBTQ+ community, there has traditionally been the feeling that the issues gay men face are taken more seriously than the issues trans people face. That is improving because we as a community are taking intersectionality into account. Similarly, there has been friction in the feminist movement because traditionally feminism has only worked for the issues white women face. Intersectional feminism attempts to address this bias. In order to be truly inclusive, we need to take intersectionality into account when we work to improve inclusion. For more information about intersectionality, please see the context included in the footnotes of this chapter or in the resources at the end of this book.

---

27 Kimberlé Crenshaw, "The Urgency of Intersectionality," *TED*, December 7, 2016, TED video, 18:41, https://www.ted.com/talks/kimberle_crenshaw_the_urgency_of_intersectionality.

Racism

Racism is prejudice plus social power. It's really as simple and as complicated as that. Now to answer your next question: can people of color be racist? It's always the next question, but it's a narrow view of the wider issue, so my answer is both a yes and a no. On the one hand, many social scientists, including Robin DiAngelo, author of *White Fragility*,[28] believe that people of color can be prejudiced against other races, but only white people have the social power to enact laws that weaponize their prejudice against other races. That impact is racism. The "powerless" definition ignores the racist views some Black people can take against other Black people. If you take a deeper view of the impact of racism within nonwhite communities, like Ibram X. Kendi, author of *Stamped*[29] and *How to Be an Antiracist*[30] does, then yes. Dr. Kendi has stated that people of color can be racist, especially those with "limited" power to enact change through antiracism.

According to Kendi, many Black people throughout history, himself included (as a teenager), have taken white supremacist views against other Black people. He says, "To say that Black people can't be racist is to say that Black people are being antiracist at all times,"[31] which is not true at all. Furthermore, to say people of color can't be racist is to let those who have limited power in government, media, academia, and other institutions off the hook for continuing racist policies, ideologies, and actions by saying they didn't have the power to enact change anyway. This is also false, and those folks should rightly be called racist. In my opinion, both things are true. I agree with Dr. Kendi that people who have the power to enact change and don't—and, in fact, repeat white supremacy—are racists, regardless of color.

28   Robin DiAngelo, *White Fragility: Why It's so Hard for White People to Talk about Racism* (Boston: Beacon Press, 2018).

29   Ibram X. Kendi, *Stamped from the Beginning* (New York: Bold Type Books, 2016).

30   Ibram X. Kendi, *How to Be an Antiracist* (New York: One World, 2019).

31   Kendi, *How to Be an Antiracist.*

I also agree that historically, no other ethnic group has had the social power to weaponize their prejudice against Black bodies specifically and people of color in general. When people of color hold prejudice against other "races," that is called prejudice; when they act out of their prejudice, it's called discrimination.

Obviously, this is a very complicated and intersectional issue with many moving pieces and would require more scholarship than I can provide here, but this book contains many resources for those who wish to learn more, provided in a resource list.

RACE/ISM:[32] Dr. Shay-Akil McLean (@hood_biologist) coined this notion when we talk about "race"[33] to indicate that the practice and ideologies of racism actually **preceded** the concept of race. Race itself is not biologically "real" in that it is a social construct that we ascribe value to, just like currency. We assign meaning to the concept of race in our society, but it has no true, scientific basis on its own. Race for the purposes of American history began to justify the crime of chattel slavery, which was intended to pass down bondage from mother to child, rather than other forms of slavery that already existed in the world.[34] That does not mean it has no power. Money has power also. That's what assigned value does; it creates rules around an idea. But according to the prolific antiracist and 50-year activist Jane Elliot, there is one race: the human race. "We've used these terms in the past; we're not going to use them in the future. Words are important. You can change a society by forcing members of that society to speak correctly. For us to continue to use words like biracial and multiracial is to accept and reinforce the idea of a number of different races. So, even with your very good friends who are proud of what they are, you need

---

32   Dr. Shay-Akil McLean, "Decolonize ALL the Things," Decolonize ALL the Things, accessed January 27, 2021, https://decolonizeallthethings.com/.

33   I use quotes around race also.

34   Dorothy E Roberts, *Fatal Invention: How Science, Politics, and Big Business Re-Create Race in the Twenty-First Century* (New York: The New Press, 2012).

to say, 'That's fine; it's a good thing to be proud of your differentness. Absolutely! But we are all the same race.'

"So let's talk about the differences as they really exist. There are 2,500 different skin colors on the face of the earth. Can you think of 2,500 different names for races? Because if you can't, you'd better start saying 'mosaic.'"[35] That does not mean you "don't see color." It means you understand that race is a social construct and there are no biological differences. But, and this is a big but, it's crucial you understand we live in a racialized society, and that means there are laws, policies, and ideas disproportionately harming people with darker skin today. Because if you "can't see color," you aren't seeing racism, and you aren't fighting for change.

Reverse Racism

Reverse racism is a term racists have coined and popularized to hide behind when people challenge their racism and privilege, and it should come as no surprise that *there is no such thing*. White supremacists fear a world where the power they have would be removed from them and given to people of color. In that case, if the entire social structure were reversed, it would still just be called racism. And even if it were to take place, it would take generations to reach the same amount of inequity toward white people that has been leveled toward Black people to this point in our history.

Colorism

The systems of white supremacy are so strong, so layered, and so insidious that Black communities can sometimes prefer lighter skin; this is called colorism. It started with slavery when children

---

35 Victoria Adelaide, "Jane Elliott," *Beautiful Humans*, July 2, 2018, https://www. beautifulhumans.info/jane-elliott/.

of rape by white masters and their slaves often had lighter skin. These children were often granted more privileges and treated with more care by their white fathers and the community, which led to a preference for lighter skin. Colorism persists to this day and has had a tremendously negative impact on the Black community and other communities of color. Not the least of which are harmful standards of beauty, where we see skin bleach being sold and used by darker-skinned people.

Cultural Appropriation

Susan Scafidi, author of *Who Owns Culture? Appropriation and Authenticity in American Law*,[36] defines cultural appropriation as "Taking intellectual property, traditional knowledge, cultural expressions, or artifacts from someone else's culture without permission. This can include unauthorized use of another culture's dance, dress, music, language, folklore, cuisine, traditional medicine, religious symbols, etc. It's most likely to be harmful when the source community is a minority group that has been oppressed or exploited in other ways or when the object of appropriation is particularly sensitive, e.g. sacred objects." For example, white women wearing Native American headdresses to Coachella or adopting a "blaccent."[37] We're also seeing "Blackfishing," (from catfishing) where white content creators on social media change everything about their natural appearance to pass themselves off as Black creators for brand sponsorships targeting Black audiences. Similarly, there have been two white women, both professors, who have been involved in scandals where it was revealed they were "pretending" to be

---

36 Susan Scafidi, *Who Owns Culture?: Appropriation and Authenticity in American Law* (New Brunswick, NJ: Rutgers University Press, 2005).
37 Adopting a "Black accent."

Black women, one on social media, and one (à la Rachel Dolezal) in her real life.

Words You Can't Say (and Why)

You already know what they are, and I'm not going to write them all down for you. For the sake of demonstration, let's discuss one in particular to illustrate the effects of how these words can dehumanize others. Recently, someone used the word "tranny" to indicate her displeasure about the presence of a particular nonbinary person in a tech group for women. When I spoke up, she brushed me off and said, "Everything you say these days is going to offend someone." Now, maybe you agree with her. Here's why you shouldn't.

This example is true for all of these off-limits words, but "tranny" specifically targets transgender people and normalizes dehumanizing them. Dehumanization has already led to outcomes where trans people are murdered at an alarming rate because they are thought of as less human. It leads to laws being weaponized against trans people by the government. It leads to horrifying suicide rates in the trans community, including trans children. Words that dehumanize people as a group have an impact on the lives of the people you disparage by spreading them. You don't get to divorce yourself from these outcomes. It's not about "being PC." Or "protecting special snowflakes." Or avoiding offending someone. By using these words, you are saying: "I am okay with those outcomes. I am okay with your suicide, I'm okay with laws that target you, I'm okay with violence against you, and I'm okay if you're murdered." If you choose to use these words, you need to also own the cost.

Deadnaming, Othering, and Pronouns

While we're here, when a trans person chooses a name for themselves that they feel matches their gender, you need to respect that. You need to celebrate that. To not do so and use someone's old name is to "deadname" them, and it's traumatic to constantly be othered[38] in that way. Especially at work. Try harder.

Pronouns: Pronouns define your gender identity so people can refer to you in the way that you prefer. Stating your pronouns in your LinkedIn profile and your email signatures means that you are normalizing doing so for people whose pronouns might be more ambiguous, and that promotes inclusivity. My pronouns are she/her/hers;[39] if you identify as male, that would be he/him/his. If you identify as nonbinary, your pronouns are likely they/them/theirs, but they don't have to be. In fact, Zoomers[40] have a whole host of pronouns they're using now[41] and that's awesome. The easiest way to ask someone what their pronouns are is to tell them yours: "I'm Di Ciruolo. My pronouns are she/her/hers." "What are you?" is never the right question, unless you're expecting the answer to be "a velociraptor."

Ableism

According to The Center for Disability Rights, Inc.,[42] ableism is a set of beliefs or practices that devalue and discriminate against people with physical, intellectual, or psychiatric differences. Policies in workplaces can be ableist; for example, harsh attendance policies that don't address disabilities or the chronically ill. Or including "walking" as an essential task in a job description when rolling would also be fine. Not having

---

38 To other someone is to separate them out from a community they would be part of. Like at work. Not using someone's name or pronouns because you don't agree puts them on the outside of the team and harms them for your comfort.

39 I also use *ella*.

40 *Zoomers* describes members of Gen Z.

41 Sakshi Venkatraman, "Beyond 'He' and 'She': 1 in 4 LGBTQ Youths Use Nonbinary Pronouns, Survey Finds," NBC News, July 30, 2020, https://www. nbcnews.com/feature/nbc-out/beyond-he-she-1-4-lgbtq-youths-use-nonbinary-pronouns-n1235204.

42 Leah Smith, "#Ableism," Center for Disability Rights, accessed January 26, 2021, http://cdrnys.org/blog/uncategorized/ableism/#:~:text=Leah%20Smith.

an accessible building, not addressing the needs of the Deaf and Hard of Hearing (HOH) community, or otherwise not educating yourself to the other communities of diversity and how much they have to offer the workforce is ableist, and we can do better. For people who are HOH, never ask if they can read lips. That puts all the responsibility for effective communication on them and again others them. Use your phone, try notes. There's an app for that.

The Model Minority Myth

This is an ethnic minority demographic group whose members are perceived to achieve a higher degree of socioeconomic success than the population average. This success is typically measured by income, education, low criminality, and high family/marital stability.[43] The Model Minority Myth is holding up Asian populations' "model," postulating that Asian Americans had "made it" in American society and thus cementing the false narrative that our current system "worked" not only for White America but Asian Americans too—so it couldn't be racist. The (false) theory was that this was because of Asian culture: hardworking and hyperintelligent. The Model Minority Myth gave rise to a plethora of problems for Asian communities. Teachers in public schools excluded Asian students from resources they might need to keep up, wrongly thinking they were naturally more gifted—even though some students did not speak English at home. Similarly, the false assumption that Asian women are demure leads to an astronomically high rate of domestic violence against them (not counting how that plays out in the workforce). Moreover, speaking of the workforce, it is far more common for Asian Americans to rise to the level of middle management and go no higher because we are still enacting these false

---

43   Crystal Tang, "Unpacking the Model Minority Myth," Beneficial State Foundation, June 4, 2019, https://beneficialstate.org/perspectives/unpacking-the-model-minority-myth/.

narratives that keep people in racist boxes. Lastly, the Model Minority Myth is weaponized against other minorities, keeping them at odds with the Asian community, when they share many of the same concerns.

Ethnicity

Ethnicity represents the pieces of culture passed down over generations and often carried to new homelands when groups of a culture move to new locations. It encompasses language, cultural belief systems, often religions, and what 23andMe calls genetic "variants."[44] When we talk about genetic testing for ancestry, we aren't testing for "race"; we're testing for data markers seen in certain pockets of the world, usually within communities of people. Sometimes this is a shared nationality but not always. For example, it's a common misconception that "race" plays a part in the appearance of diseases. Dorothy Roberts[45] retells a true story to NPR of an African American girl being in and out of the emergency room throughout her life for lung-related illnesses; by the time she was eight, a doctor finally thought to give her a chest X-ray, and the radiologist remarked (without knowing the child's "race"), "Who's the kid with cystic fibrosis?" If the child had been Caucasian, the doctors would have diagnosed her with cystic fibrosis in infancy, because cystic fibrosis tends to appear more often in Caucasian children.[46] Similarly, many Caucasian patients have presented with sickle cell symptoms to doctors unaware such a thing is possible. Sickle cell affects people with ancestry in North Africa or the Mediterranean. That's not a racial group. See how understanding the difference between ethnicity—which is a real thing—and race (which is a social construct) has serious impact?

---

44 "The Science behind 23andMe," 23andMe, accessed January 26, 2021, https://www.23andme.com/genetic-science/.

45 Author of *Fatal Invention*.

46 Dorothy Roberts, Dorothy Roberts: What's Race Got to Do with Medicine?, interview by Guy Raz, NPR, February 7, 2017, https://www.npr.org/transcripts/514150399.

Hispanic vs. Latinx

People of color is a broad term that mostly means "everyone who isn't white." When I talk about racism, in fact when most people talk about racism, we're talking about the most observable example, which is *anti-Blackness*, and working from there. That doesn't mean other people don't exist or that they don't experience racism; they definitely do. We also perpetuate a lot of prejudice within our own communities, which again stems from white supremacy and colonialism. Hispanic and Latinx (la-teen-x) are not the same thing. *Hispanic* is a term used to describe people whose ancestry originates in countries that are Spanish-speaking. That's from Mexico through South America with the exception of Brazil, because Brazilians, thanks to colonialism, speak Portuguese. Hispanic also includes Spain and (as of the 2013 U.S. census) Portugal. I know, they speak Portuguese in Portugal too, but the U.S. has a complicated relationship with "race" mostly because it's an entirely made-up concept. Historically, Hispanic people were considered white until around 1930, when white people were like, "Nah."[47]

It's gotten more absurd throughout the years. Latinx means everyone who comes from a Latin country, which is Mexico all the way south through Brazil. However, it does not include Spain and Portugal.[48] About half of Spain identifies as white; the other largest group is "mestizo," which means mixed. The reason we say "Latinx" and not "Latino" is because Spanish is a gendered (Romance) language and basically, in English, we've stopped saying "he" to mean he/she/they. The "x" is an effort to be inclusive by removing the gendered limitations of the Spanish language. That being said, not everyone is interested in being called "Latinx" because of prejudice stemming from white supremacy.

---

47 U.S. Department of Commerce, "We the American...Hispanics," *Census.gov* (September 1993), https://www.census.gov/prod/cen1990/wepeople/we-2r.pdf.
48 "The colonizers" as some have rightly argued, but that exchange went both ways.

In fact, you'll find a lot of Latinx families that will brag about their "European" heritage and will still largely prefer white beauty standards. Check out the social movement canceling "Latinidad" on that. Those folks, in my experience, prefer the term "Hispanic."

Other news you can use: There was also a racist effort in Latin countries post-colonialism called *"Blanqueamiento"*—literally "whitening"—which was a racist effort that was intended to *mejorar la raza,* or improve the race. White Europeans were resettled in Latin countries for this reason. Totally real, look it up.[49] Now, there are Latinx or Hispanic individuals from all "races"; White, Asian, Indigenous, and African (which, notably, is called "Afro-Latinx") and so forth. Hispanic and Latinx people exist in every skin color, even if there is very little representation of that in the media. Individuals will often identify based on their country of origin as opposed to/or in addition to "Hispanic" or "Latinx."[50] As a general rule, let people identify themselves; don't try to correct them or stuff them into identity boxes that don't fit them for your understanding or comfort.

TL;DR:

- White supremacy and racism are systemic, and allies must dismantle them in order to move the needle forward.
- You aren't color-blind. It's disingenuous to claim you are—no one believes you, and worst of all, you're likely to have **more** biases and blind spots by thinking this a nonissue for you, not fewer.

---

49 Tanya Katerí Hernández, "Colorism and the Law in Latin America—Global Perspectives on Colorism Conference Remarks," *Washington University Global Studies Law Review* 14, no. 4 (2015): 683–93, https://openscholarship.wustl.edu/cgi/viewcontent.cgi?article=1551&context=law_globalstudies.

50 Graciela Mochkofsky, "Who Are You Calling Latinx?," *New Yorker*, September 5, 2020, https://www.newyorker.com/news/daily-comment/who-are-you-calling-.latinx

- Stereotype threat is insidious and leads to negative impact for URGs in work situations, especially job interviews. Priming stereotypes makes these outcomes worse.
- Work hard to address intersectionality in your inclusion work.
- Allyship is **knowledge** plus **understanding** plus **action**.[51]
- There are more forms of diversity in the workforce than skin color, gender, and sexual orientation—let's do the work to educate ourselves for true inclusivity.
- The Model Minority Myth harms people of Asian descent and repeats racist narratives to the benefit of white supremacy.
- Latinx and Hispanic aren't the same thing. Let people identify themselves, and don't try to force them into identity boxes that don't fit them for *your* comfort.

---

51 Rachel Cargle, "The Great Unlearn," Patreon, accessed January 26, 2021, https://www.patreon.com/thegreatunlearn/posts.

PART 1

CREATING A CULTURE THAT PROMOTES DIVERSITY, EQUITY, AND INCLUSION

"So how are you guys attracting and retaining more-diverse talent?" This is the question I asked the woman across the table from me, over coffee in 2018. I really wanted to work with her company—let's call it Ranger—and had offered a free consultation. "Ranger" is a software as a service (SaaS) company, a marketing powerhouse with more than 3,000 employees worldwide. I was impressed by its commitment to diversity, equity, and inclusion, and I wanted to learn and grow in a place that shared my values. It is consistently recognized by Glassdoor's "Best Places to Work" award, and I love its brand.

"We aren't," said the woman (who served as Ranger's Head of People), matter of factly.

I responded with my surprise; I'd seen so many posts about Ranger's initiatives and the pictures of happy, diverse employees. She slowly sipped her coffee, clearly measuring her words before deciding to just be honest: "It's marketing." *Obviously.* Ranger's marketing was geared toward attracting more-diverse candidates. But when such new hires arrived, I later learned, they discovered the same problems they'd experienced at so many other companies. This was causing a high turnover rate and, even worse, a lack of diverse representation at the top.

"And it *is* a great place to work, of course," the woman continued. "I mean, we really do care. None of us see color." *Another one of these,* I thought—a business with its own staffing team seeking a free consultation before claiming to conduct its own diversity initiatives internally. When I later spoke to a Hispanic woman they'd interviewed, she said: "I really did want to work with them, but I felt like they were putting me up for a job I wasn't qualified for just to check a diversity box." Ranger, I learned, had already decided to hire a white man before interviewing her. Why would a well-intentioned company do that?

Well, it happens all the time. Many large tech companies want to be seen making diversity and inclusion a priority, so they hire someone to solve all their internal and systemic problems, while granting them no power to make change. Later that same quarter, when the problems are still there, these companies will reach out to "pick my brain," and here we are. They're all adopting the Rooney Rule, created by the NFL to require teams to interview ethnic minorities before filling a senior coaching position. It can be a great thing—and it can also go sideways, as it had with Ranger.

This is just one example of a company with good "diversity" policies—but no allyship. You can have the absolute best diversity officer in the business instituting the best practices, but without a culture that promotes allyship, you've solved nothing. Without allyship, nothing changes. Without a willingness to change and learn and do better, everything stays the same.

As the research and stories in the following chapters reveal, we're still a long way from creating cultures that promote DEI,[52] no matter what their branding and marketing tells you. I'll also share strategies

---

52 Diversity, Equity & Inclusion

for combining diversity policies with allyship to create a true culture of DEI.

Chapter 1
DIVERSITY VALUES ARE DEVALUED

Recently, researchers David R. Hekman and Stefanie K. Johnson surveyed 350 executives on "diversity-valuing" behaviors.[53] They found women+ and nonwhite managers who promoted other women and nonwhite employees were thought to be less competent by their own managers.

But white men who promoted women and other URGs were not thought to be less competent. This study was run twice with the same results. According to Johnson and Hekman: "Basically, all managers were judged harshly if they hired someone who looked like them, unless they were a white male." So white men can not only hire other white men with no adverse effects to their career; they can also hire and promote the rest of us.

Why is knowing this fact important? Because more women+ and URGs in a company won't change the culture without white men as

---

53 Stefanie K. Johnson and David R. Hekman, "Women and Minorities Are Penalized for Promoting Diversity," *Harvard Business Review*, March 23, 2016, https://hbr.org/2016/03/women-and-minorities-are-penalized-for-promoting-diversity.

5

allies. We need white men to step up, step forward, and participate in making the changes that need to be made in tech and other STEM fields. Look, if any one of us could change the whole system ourselves, we would! But we can't do it alone. It really is that simple.

> *"People are opting out of vital conversations about diversity and inclusivity because they fear looking wrong, saying something wrong, or being wrong. Choosing our own comfort over hard conversations is the epitome of privilege, and it corrodes trust and moves us away from meaningful and lasting change."*
> —**Brené Brown** in *Dare to Lead*, explaining one of the 10 behaviors and cultural issues leaders identified as getting in our way in organizations around the world.

Tech Talk

I've consulted extensively in the tech industry, and I can tell you firsthand, it's a mess. In interview after interview, women and URGs have shared stories of workplaces trying to look more like the stereotypes reinforced by HBO's *Silicon Valley* projecting squeaky-clean shots of women and people of color at the top. Most recently, this issue hit the front page of everyone's awareness with the mainstreaming of the Black Lives Matter, or BLM, movement. Many companies were coming out for the first time in support of Black Lives Matter, but they seemed to be following a "trend." After George Floyd's murder, Salesforce was one of the first out of the gate. But it's extremely important to note that other companies like Ben & Jerry's were way ahead of the curve with their own BLM statement— by years. According to Mita Mallick, then Head of Diversity and Cross-Cultural Marketing at Unilever, "Sometimes, you just need to come out on the right side of history and wait for other people to catch up."

As more eyes turned toward tech as the movement spread, we learned that all of the top tech companies *did* have at least one person of color at the table, and that person usually had the same title: "Chief of Diversity." During that same time, those of us in the DEI field watched while companies took whomever among them *looked* the most diverse and put them in charge of diversity with no additional compensation or support. It became their responsibility to bear the entire weight of the systemic problems they were directly impacted and victimized by from the start of their career there. Are you seeing the problem with this yet? You will.

Similarly, many companies are creating employee resource groups (ERGs) to involve employees who have experienced these systemic problems and give them a voice to address these concerns in a safe space. Speaking to the *Washington Post* on the subject, Dominique Hollins, veteran of Google and eBay, said: "The dependence on ERGs has stifled the industry because it gives a false sense of progress. We joined the ERG because we needed help, but we became the help."[54]

Look, I'm a big fan of ERGs, and I think they can do a lot of good in a company, especially when it comes to keeping leaders honest and up to date on the issues and policies directly impacting their employees. (See my advice at the end of this chapter.) In fact, I help leaders form them in start-ups as advisory groups. But ERGs can't be leading the fight for an inclusive workforce. They can't shoulder the burden of improving the culture of an oppressive workplace—that's what a DEI professional is for. ERGs can't be solely responsible for attracting diverse talent—that's what staffing professionals do. They can't be used as props at conferences like Grace Hopper or AfroTech—that is the responsibility of leadership. If you want to be an ally, you have to do

54   Nitasha Tiku, "Tech Companies Are Asking Their Black Employee Groups to Fix Silicon Valley's Race Problem — Often for Free," *Washington Post*, June 26, 2020, https://www.washingtonpost.com/technology/2020/06/26/black-ergs-tech/.

the *real* work. Anything else is performative allyship: a performance with no real impact or substance.

Or as Jenni Lee of Statisfy said better: "Hey, Google, thanks, but your efforts to bring more women into tech is really just tokenism. Instead of throwing money at the problem (i.e., paying for a few women to take coding classes or putting them up at nice hotels at women's only conferences), you should just give them a dignified job. Put your money where your PR is."[55]

Let's look at some numbers for a moment. According to the Holloway Report's "Diversity and Inclusion in Tech," women make up 57% of the U.S. workforce as a whole, but only 26% of the technical workforce. Black, Latina, and Native American women make up 16% of the U.S. workforce and hold only 4% of tech jobs. And only 10% of tech executives are women, write Jennifer Wong and Jason Kim.

Asian and Asian American men make up 32% of the tech workforces, but only 20% hold executive positions. While Asian and Asian American women make up 15% of the workforce, they hold only 5% of executive roles in tech.[56]

"Harassment and discrimination," write Wong and Kim, "affect workers based on their caregiver status, immigration status, gender identity, sexual orientation, and disability status."

There was this "uniform" that everyone wore, which was a Patagonia vest, and everyone who wore one seemed to have this "brogramming" attitude. The engineers walked around as if

---

55 Jenni Lee, "What Young Women in Tech Really Need," in *Lean Out: The Struggle for Gender Equality in Tech and Startup Culture*, ed. Elissa Shevinsky (New York, NY: OR Books, 2015), 174.

56 Jennifer Kim and Jason Wong, "Diversity and Inclusion in Tech, Part 1: Foundations, Myths, and Pitfalls," *Holloway*, December 5, 2019, https://www.holloway.com/s/trh-excerpt-diversity-and-inclusion-in-tech-pt-1-foundations-myths-and-pitfalls.

they were incapable of being wrong, and I didn't fit in. Some women, who were friends and felt I was an ally, had reported to me that they were being targeted for sexual harassment by one of the engineering managers. I begged them to report him, but they were scared. No one wanted to be singled out by the team or thought of as a traitor or a troublemaker or someone who couldn't take a joke. No one wanted their careers ruined. It would have been a breach of their trust to report him, so I didn't do anything about it.

Later that same year, there was a gay male manager who would get drunk at get-togethers and sexually assault guys who worked there. He was pretty high up in the food chain, and everyone was talking about it, and how if he tries to touch you, you should let him so he can help your career and not ruin it. At one party, he walked up to a guy and grabbed him in the junk right in front of someone from HR. When the guy who had been grabbed stood up for himself and reported to HR, and only after an HR rep had been a witness, guess who got a golden parachute? The predator. He was given a huge severance to quit and not sue the company. He's at another company now.

—A.G., large online discount furniture retailer

There are glimmers of hope, which you'll read about at the end of this book. When I began interviewing one nationwide tech school, I was thrilled to learn how the leadership team had been making thoughtful changes affecting the entire company culture for the better. There's now a Slack channel dedicated to DEI, where everyone's invited to contribute on policies and how each is respectful (or not) of their diversity of people. They host girls' coding events, contribute to the local diversity fabric and form relationships with Historically Black Colleges and Universities (HBCUs) and Predominantly Black

Institutions (PBIs). They mentor women+ and URGs and help them network, providing sponsorship.

Still, leaders must learn to both reach out to more-diverse groups and lean into the untapped potential of their company. Aubrey Blanche, a designer of equitable organizations and products at Culture Amp and a diversity thought leader, writes on Medium how the tech industry has done a terrible job of recruiting and retaining people who don't come from a very small set of backgrounds. "From social and economic factors that influence who is given access to computers," she writes, "to being constantly—overtly or implicitly—questioned about your suitability for a career in tech, members of groups underrepresented in tech face significant additional barriers to entering and staying in tech than their well-represented counterparts."[57]

Blanche continues to discuss the so-called pipeline problem blamed for the tech industry's lack of diversity, adding more statistics to those from the Holloway Report. As she points out, 11% of technical degrees go to Black and Hispanic students, but most tech workforces include only 2% to 3% people of color. "Simply put," writes Blanche, "before we can meaningfully talk about a 'pipeline problem,' we have to effectively employ the pipeline that already exists."

And that can be a tough task when people are promoting toxic cultures and jamming up the pipeline with discriminatory behaviors and processes.

I've been working at a SaaS-focused marketing agency for about two years (due to our turnover, I'm now in the top 10% of folks in terms of seniority). Since the first few months, I flagged to my

---

57   Aubrey Blanche, "Diversity 101: The Barriers to Diversity across the Pipeline," Medium, January 17, 2017, https://medium.com/@adblanche/diversity-101-the-barrier-to-gender-diversity-across-the-pipeline-c0437dc57960.

then-manager (our now-COO) my interest in advancing up a track to a department head for technical, dev-focused content. Got all kinds of encouragement that they were grooming me for this role, etc.

About a year ago, a very junior guy joined our team. He was assigned as my second hand for one of my clients, and I trained/mentored him for a few months before he was given his own account (which I took as a good thing, like, "Hey I trained them well, they're competent. Yay!"). Since then, the opportunities I'm given to work on my track have dramatically decreased, and largely have been diverted to him. He's still junior to me, and every one of his technical clients have churned (while I've kept most of them, many of which have reupped with us). He's treated like an expert in dev-focused content, and our CEO defers to him for leading a how-to-do-dev-content-well program, even though I'm the one with hands-on coding experience and a track record of running these clients well, not to mention management experience.

The icing on the cake is that the same day this junior employee hit me up to get on a Zoom call to "consult" on his program, our CEO (a person I've known for two years since they were a direct manager) quoted some work of mine from my side project and spelled my name incorrectly in a company-wide memo. I can't help feeling like my experience, presence at the company, and knowledge is being discounted in favor of yet another young white dude in tech who fails upward. It's demoralizing, to say the least; every junior white guy seems to be treated like a rising star who will never need to go on maternity leave by management. Everywhere.

—C.F., SaaS marketing company

TL;DR:

- We need white men to step up, step forward, and participate in making the changes that need to be made in tech and other STEM fields.
- The dependence on creating ERGs without committing to systemic improvements has stifled the industry because it displays a false sense of progress.
- Women make up 57% of the U.S. workforce as a whole, but only 26% of the technical workforce. Black, Latina, and Native American women make up 16% of the U.S. workforce and hold only 4% of tech jobs. And only 10% of tech executives are women.

Chapter 2

THE WORKING-OVER
OF WORKING MOMS

When I was 30, my partner and I became pregnant, and I was terrified. I had just started a few months earlier at an almost entirely male biotech company in Cambridge, and I was worried about how that would go. When I was nine weeks along, I told my boss I was pregnant. It was well before I should have been telling people, but I was trying to be forthcoming. A few days later, he pulled me into his office to "discuss my issue." It turned out that he—along with the leadership team of all white men—had met to discuss what was to be done about my pregnancy. Obviously, without consulting me. "We've decided to support you," he declared proudly. "Make sure you call Mike and thank him." I nodded, dazed, and left. *Support me?! Support me with what?* Had firing me been on the table? I would later find out the answer to that was very much "yes," and the company founder (a white man in his sixties) felt as if I'd gotten away with something—joining and then becoming pregnant on purpose. That company no longer exists, and I'll bet it's at least partially due to attitudes like this.

What happened to the promise of inclusive cultures for working mothers? And yes, I do write *mothers* here instead of parents, and you'll soon see why. More than 70% of American women with children under 18 work, according to the Bureau of Labor Statistics. That should merit a bit of attention to their unique needs in the workplace, no? (I'm talking breastfeeding with dignity, not shame; flex hours to take care of kids; acknowledging their productivity, etc.)

Nope! In "Working Mothers Are the Backbone of the U.S. Economy: So why are they still treated like morally bankrupt second-class citizens?" *Dame* magazine writer Caroline Shannon-Karasik discusses the "motherhood penalty," or the decrease in a woman's income once she becomes a mother. She points to one survey of more than 2,400 economists showing that mothers are actually more productive than their child-free counterparts.[58]

"Mothers of at least two children are, on average, more productive than mothers of only one child, and mothers, in general, are more productive than childless women," noted the study. "Fathers of at least two children are also more productive than fathers of one child and childless men."

But women see a 4% decrease in pay per child born or adopted, writes Shannon-Karasik, compared to a 6% jump in income for dads—the "fatherhood bonus."

"Momming" Shenanigans

One woman with the initials J.L. working in academia shared her plight with me. When it comes to mothers, the attitude is, "We should be grateful that Company X is willing to put up with our needing to

---

58   Matthias Krapf, Heinrich W. Ursprung, and Christian Zimmermann, "Parenthood and Productivity of Highly Skilled Labor: Evidence from the Groves of Academe," *Federal Reserve Bank of St. Louis Working Paper Series* 2014-001A (2014), https://doi.org/10.20955/wp.2014.001.

leave for doctors' appointments and not being able to accommodate last-minute meetings because we need a babysitter," said J.L. "I've also found that every time I've asked for some advancement, I've been told no until I pushed back and had some leverage. Every single time, and I've been working professionally for ten years."

She shared the gist and timeline of conversations from her last job.

Winter 2018

J.L.: "Hey, I'm feeling really overwhelmed, and this isn't a great fit for me anymore. What about moving to part-time?"

Company X: "No way, this is a full-time position."

Spring 2019 (when J.L. was working every weekend, getting asked to work more, and caring for her daughter, who was hospitalized for pneumonia).

J.L.: "This isn't workable for me anymore. I resign."

Company X: "Oh nooooo, but we really like you and value your work. Okay, I guess we'll let you work part-time."

J.L.: "That's great, thanks, but I just want to give you a heads up that this won't be financially doable for me long term. What about the possibility of a contractor position?"

Company X: "No way. We don't do that."

Fall 2019

J.L.: Hey, this is just a heads up that I accepted a part-time contracting position with Company Y.

Company X: "Uh, so...are you quitting?"

J.L.: "Not yet, but this isn't financially doable for me long term, so I'll probably be out by the summer."

Company X: "Well maaaaaybe we could do a contracting position."

But the contracting position never happened, and J.L. left Company X.

"This is just one of these very insidious things that I see all the time," said J.L. "There's no one in a woman's corner when she wants to advance. No one. The narrative is always the same. Be grateful that we'll even keep you around with your 'momming' shenanigans."

Dads, Please, We're Drowning

You ask, "Okay, so Di, how do we do better for moms?" Well, you don't seem to have a problem with dads, right? I mean, a male friend of mine received paid leave when he adopted a *dog*. I'm not hating on fur kids or their parents. Do your thing, but the problem with being a mother in tech or STEM is the fact that it's stigmatized, not that we exist.

I'll give you an example: I was lurking on LinkedIn (I basically follow the rest of the DEI community), and I saw a post shared by David L. Casey, who's amazing. He's the VP of Workforce Strategies and CDO for CVS; the post was by a dad who was speaking to other dads about having children. I'm paraphrasing, but basically Dad volunteered to be the guest reader at his daughter's preschool before naptime. He talks about how delighted she was (aw!), and how he checked the sign-up sheet and realized none of the other dads had signed up! Dad himself didn't even know you *could* volunteer! He concludes by telling the other dads, "Time is fleeting. Work will be there when you get back; take the time to be there with your kids."

Now, that's a great message. Of course it is. Here's what Dad missed: you know who knew that you needed to volunteer at preschool? Mom.[59] You know who probably *did* volunteer and had to lie to her boss about an appointment, miss a meeting, and get penalized at work for prioritizing

---

59 Now, if you're thinking *This is heteronormative*, I agree. Of course it is. I'm not saying this is the only problem by calling it out, and I'm not saying it's the most important. I'm saying this is still going on, and it's keeping moms out of the workforce, and that's a big problem.

that fleeting time with the kids? Mom. Who gets to be thought of as less committed and less competent by her managers and peers? Mom. What Dad needed to do was talk to other dads about *normalizing* prioritizing fleeting time with kids for *all* of us, not just dads. Get there, dads; we need you at the frontlines. Please. We're drowning.

The Pandemic and Parenting

Nobody knows when (or even if) COVID-19 will fully retreat from our lives. (*Gulp.*) I love kids, and I really love my kids, but most of you working parents will agree: this situation is driving us insane, and it's absolutely untenable. This pandemic is highlighting huge gaps in privilege, where many companies are happy to have you as long as you can manage to work from home with kids while you have no access to childcare. At one point, Florida State University has announced a return to the old policy of parents not being allowed to work from home while watching their kids, as before, but later backtracked after facing backlash. After all, how did they expect parents to return to the workforce when work wasn't safe and no daycares were open...? Similarly, a friend of mine just told me that all the parents with school-aged children at her job were fired for being "less productive." I asked her how we knew that; "Where's the data? How are they getting away with that?" According to the company, it was the pandemic. It's the assumption from bias.

A study by Catalyst, a global nonprofit supporting the advancement of women+ in the workplace, shows a huge divide between how employees think the pandemic will affect inclusion and how company leaders think the pandemic will affect inclusion.[60]

---

60   Catalyst, "Catalyst Workplace Survey Reveals Optimism about Gender Equity during Covid-19, but Skepticism on Commitment of Companies," Catalyst, June 30, 2020, https://www.catalyst.org/media-release/workplace-gender-equity-covid-19./

"Business leaders are more likely than employees to believe that COVID-19 provides companies with an opportunity to create more inclusive workplaces for women (75% vs. 60%)," write the authors. "Business leaders are also more likely to believe that working remotely has facilitated a more inclusive environment (56% vs. 28%). There is also a division in perception of company action—business leaders (56%) are more likely to believe that their company is taking steps to enhance gender equity during this pandemic, as compared with employees (34%)."

That goals-versus-realities division exists in the lives of employees working from home as well, especially as it relates to women+ in the workforce.

Domestic gender[61] roles at home:
- A third of men claim to have taken on more of the household chores, suggesting a leveling of roles and responsibilities, but only 13% of women say that their male partner has taken on more of the household chores.[62]
- Women are twice as likely as men to be primarily responsible for homeschooling their children.

Virtual meetings:
- Of women business leaders, 45% say it's difficult for women to speak up in virtual meetings. (And 42% of men business leaders agree with this observation.)

---

61 "This gender difference reported is based on men and women living with an opposite-sex partner. Among same-sex couples, 3 in 10 working men say they are doing more household chores since the work-from-home orders were put in place. Among women in same-sex partnerships, the balance is more equal, with 1 in 4 working women doing more at home, yet 1 in 4 saying their female partner is doing more." Catalyst, "Catalyst Workplace Survey."

62 Collective *snort* noted.

- One-fifth of women recently felt ignored and overlooked by coworkers during video calls, and one-fifth of working people have witnessed more discrimination at work since the outbreak of COVID-19.

While I've found no research on new company policies for working parents, I was encouraged by reading a recent story in *Forbes* about how the tide may be turning. Quoting Agnes Uhereczky, the Executive Director of the WorkLife HUB based in Belgium, Tracy Brower writes, "The pandemic has shone a light on the more subtle forms of diversity, such as whether somebody is a parent or a caregiver."

As Brower explains, video conferencing gives us a rare window into people's lives and homes—where children may be playing in the background. Some employees may need more time to care for a sick parent. "Many leaders are expanding their empathy and compassion for employees," she writes, "as they face more work–life challenges themselves and see firsthand the obstacles their employees face."

Leaders are still grappling with long-term implications for DEI, and from my interviews, still need to address allyship for a truly inclusive culture as we adjust to "the new normal." As much as it stinks to work from home with family distractions, people are clearly catching on to the other benefits of flex hours.

According to another study by Catalyst,[63] the following actions can promote inclusion during this global pandemic:

1. **Lead inclusively through crisis.**

   Successful leadership during times of extreme uncertainty and ambiguity requires a foundation of inclusion built with

---

63 Catalyst, "COVID-19: Women, Equity, and Inclusion in the Future of Work," May 28, 2020.

vision, courage, clear communication, diversity, equity, transparency, and resilience.

2. **Tackle inequities.**

Broad and entrenched social inequities have been exacerbated and magnified; companies that diminish these divisions in their workplaces position themselves for greater success.

3. **Connect with empathy.**

Empathy helps bond colleagues together and sets the foundation for an integrated and inclusive workplace.

4. **Trust your team.**

Trust—involving team members as decision-makers and contributors—is a key element of inclusion and a catalyst for team empowerment.

5. **Work remotely and flexibly.**

With more disruptions inevitable, learning how to work remotely and flexibly is a business-continuity necessity and inclusion accelerator.

TL;DR:

- Mothers and fathers are more productive than childless employees. But women see a 4% decrease in pay per child born or adopted compared to a 6% jump in income for dads. It's called the "fatherhood bonus."

- Dads need to talk to other dads about prioritizing time with kids, regardless of the parent's gender. Get there, dads; your partners need you at the frontlines. Please. We're drowning.

- There's a huge divide between how *employees* think the COVID-19 pandemic will affect inclusion and how *company leaders* think the pandemic will affect inclusion.

Chapter 3

HOW EMPLOYERS CAN BUILD MORE
INCLUSIVE WORK CULTURES

M y friend Stevie is a back-end developer whose social justice core has made him passionate about inclusion in tech. He doesn't fit in any traditional identity boxes and fights against them in general. Stevie is one of the cooler people I know, and earlier this year he asked me for a favor. He was working with a start-up, was asked to bring in another developer, and had someone in mind—a nonbinary person. Stevie wanted me to check in with the owners, Tom and Ted, to see if this would be a safe space for his friend.

So I set up a meeting with the cofounders, who were in the restaurant space. After exchanging pleasantries and discussing a little about what I do, we got into it.

Tom and Ted quickly and semisheepishly explained their team was entirely made up of white guys. Entirely white, Jewish guys, specifically. I thought maybe this was a situation where these two friends had hired within their network and perhaps were looking to build from there. This is pretty common in the start-up world, where guys who went to school together or worked together at a previous company go off and spin up a company. That usually doesn't lead to the best starting point for diversity, but they were ahead of me and assured me that was not the case.

"We care about diversity, but these hires were just the best guys for the job!" Tom said. Ted agreed, nodding emphatically. But as he sat with it a moment, he followed with, "You think we just hired Jewish guys because we're Jewish guys, right?"

Now, while you might be thinking *Heck, yeah!* that wasn't my response. Instead, I said: "I think you're hiring in your network. Hiring people who share your identity and calling it 'culture fit.' Your workforce diversity goals should represent your local area and your customer base. You're in New York. Also, this isn't a situation where you're hiring for one position. You're suggesting that these folks who are entirely like you are the best fit across many positions. I just want you to be honest with yourselves and consider whether or not that is absolutely true."

While Ted paused, considering what I'd said, Tom doubled down. "Well, actually, it's because Jewish people tend to be property owners!" While I mentally planned to follow up with that comment, Ted interrupted, joking: "The restaurant industry is very diverse, but Spanish people are the worst when it comes to racism! You're Hispanic; you know that's true! Everyone hates the Cubans!" I held up my hand, realizing that we had just gone from zero to useless, and the only way to salvage the conversation was to change tactics.

"Look," I said. "The problem with hiring an entire team that's 'like you' is that you all share a lot of overlap with how you view the world and how you solve problems. It creates echo chambers. It might be comfortable, but comfort is the death of innovation. As a start-up in tech, you need to correct that. It will be a matter of life and death for you. If you don't think you can be beaten out by a more diverse and innovative team with a different idea that speaks to your customer base, I'd like to introduce you to Blockbuster."

Ted sat back in his chair, stunned. "See now, now this matters. Now you're telling me something that matters. Now this is impacting my money." I waited patiently to see if Tom was back on board, but he wasn't, and that was okay. Ted continued, "So where do we start fixing this?"

Psychological Safety

I work with tech start-ups all the time. In some cases, diversity and inclusion are an afterthought, and they're only calling on me because they're having big hiring problems, big culture problems, or some kind of discriminatory scandal. But in some really special cases, a team comes together through mutual respect of each other, and that drives the company, bringing in other people who see that the team has something special. It's not always the product or the idea. You can have a great product and a terrible company. One of my teams now has no trouble recruiting. In fact, women+ developers are on the waitlist to join when they get more funding. Inclusive teams help drive diverse hiring and great products. When people are working at a place where they belong, they invite other awesome people they know, and then I never worry about them in terms of where they're going with their product because I trust and respect the team. I know that together, they can do awesome things. There's a line from *A Knight's Tale* that has always spoken to me when it comes to leadership on teams and in companies, and when I see inclusive and high-performing teams, I'm often reminded of it: "Your men love you. If I knew nothing else about you, that would be enough."[64]

A recent team success study by Google found that "*Who* is on a team matters less than how the team members interact, structure their

---

64   *A Knight's Tale*, directed by Brian Helgeland (Columbia Pictures, 2001).

work, and view their contributions."[65] Google's study determined five key factors that predict success on teams—psychological safety, dependability, structure and clarity, meaning, and impact. But the number one factor at the core of all the others was psychological safety.

What is psychological safety? According to a study published in 1999 by Amy Edmondson, psychological safety is when a team feels safe to make mistakes and take interpersonal risks. Basically, you won't be punished when you make a mistake. Edmondson studied 51 workplaces and concluded: "As predicted, learning behavior mediates between team psychological safety and team performance. The results support an integrative perspective in which both team structures, such as context support and team leader coaching, and shared beliefs shape team outcomes."[66]

What does psychological safety have to do with building a more inclusive team? Absolutely everything. Maybe you have an employee referral program in place at your office that's been slow to yield any promising results. You may have convinced yourself that while you're interested in having employees who are women+ and people of color, they just aren't that interested in you. Before you decide that all these efforts have been fruitless, take a look at how your existing teams run. Are they inclusive? Does your team trust their managers? How's your turnover? What does your management training program look like— does it have inclusion training? If a candidate walks into your office, are they seeing themselves represented? Are they talking to employees who can answer their questions about how someone like them can expect

65   Julia Rozovsky, "The Five Keys to a Successful Google Team," re:Work, November 17, 2015, https://rework.withgoogle.com/blog/five-keys-to-a-successful-google-team/.

66   Amy Edmondson, "Psychological Safety and Learning Behavior in Work Teams," *Administrative Science Quarterly* 44, no. 2 (June 1999): 350–83, https://doi.org/10.2307/2666999.

to be treated? If your candidate is nonbinary, and they ask to use the bathroom, do you have nongendered bathrooms?

The Good Ones: Men Who Have Empowered Me as a Woman in Tech
By Loe Lee, Design Manager, HubSpot[67]

There has been a lot of horrible news floating around about how women are treated in tech. While I've experienced my fair share of sexism (pinched from behind while walking up stairs, looked up and down, etc.), I wanted to take a minute to reflect on the people—the men, in particular—who have made my work life an incredibly safe and comfortable one. I felt this way before I got pregnant. Now that I'm a mom-to-be, I have an even deeper sense of gratitude for my respectful, compassionate male colleagues.

Here are the men I'm grateful for in my career:

Robert, Senior VP and Cofounder: Robert was an executive who walked around wearing the same Cal button-down, khaki shorts, and sandals every day. His wiry gray hair was always trying to escape his head, and he approached everything with a healthy dose of playfulness and suspicion. I started my tech career as the company's administrative assistant. From day one, Robert treated me with collegial respect. We'd talk about politics at my desk. A cofounder and PhD from Cal, Robert was someone I held in incredibly high regard. When he wanted to hear what I had to say I, by default, felt smart and worthy.

---

67   Loe Lee, "The Good Ones: Men Who Have Empowered Me as a Woman in Tech," *Hi Loe Lee* (blog), February 17, 2017, http://www.hiloelee.com/blog/2017/2/25/the-good-ones. Reprinted with permission from the author.

David, Product & UX Designer: Dave is the reason I went into design. His friends were all designers, and he loved his job. I couldn't believe there was this world of thoughtful, kind people who make great money studying computers and human behavior. I told Dave I was interested in becoming a designer, and he was immediately on board. I had no product or design experience, and he helped me construct a long-term action plan to break into the field. He never questioned my ability to learn, and he willingly nurtured my curiosity as soon as it was detected.

Robert, CEO: Robert is a free-spirited hippie turned CEO. He's always laughing and adventuring. He brought me on board in my first (and possibly last?) product management role and quickly promoted me to manage the entire four-person product team. I was petrified by the responsibility, but I accepted it because Rob believed in me and gave me the chance. I attended my first board meetings and managed my first team. I managed a department budget for the first time and oversaw development processes for a 20-person team in Bangladesh. It was one of the most challenging roles I've ever had, but I learned and grew a ton. It made me a better designer.

Jeff, Tech Lead: While I'm only five months into this company, Jeff has already left an impression on me. He's a dad of three, and he has a ton of experience leading teams of engineers. I was intimidated by his experience level when I joined and that quickly dissipated as I worked with him and another 27-year-old female product manager. Jeff immediately trusted me and the PM, supporting my PM's strategic decisions and working through problems with us in an informative, respectful way. He encouraged my PM to lead, and he never made me feel stupid or inexperienced despite his greater wisdom. Jeff made it seem normal to be a young woman leading a team, and I appreciated that. It became normal for me too.

Jay, Senior Software Engineer: Jay made my jaw drop when I joined HubSpot. I remember I was in a user research meeting with him, and we were debriefing on a session we had just listened in on. There were about 10 of us in the room, and a young twentysomething woman was leading the session. Jay and the meeting leader spoke at the same time. Immediately, the woman apologized and told Jay to continue speaking. Jay paused and said, "No—this is your meeting, you go." I literally thought I stumbled into a different dimension. I had never seen a guy be so self-aware and supportive of a woman leading a meeting.

Jonathan, Design Lead: I may be drinking the Kool-Aid, but Jonathan has been the best manager I've ever had. He spends most of our 1:1s listening, and when we problem-solve together, it's always highly collaborative and rarely someone with more power telling someone with less power to do something. He advocates for his people and does it with finessed communication and no ego. He has also followed up with me frequently to ensure I'm getting what I need to do my job well while I simultaneously grow a human being. It's so helpful to have a manager who's also a new dad with a two-year-old son.

Tim, Director of Product Research and Design: When I interviewed for a new job this time around, Tim stood out in a huge way because unlike other executives/department heads, Tim listened. Most of the interview was listening. Since then,

Tim has continued to listen, and I've been incredibly touched by how compassionate and caring he is toward his people. He's an open book who cares about both good design/product and bettering the world at large.

Why are they awesome?

When I look back on these men who have nurtured my career, six of the seven are fathers. If you're looking to foster healthier, more equal work environments, maybe start there? From my experience, dads do it right.

How Employees Can Build More Inclusive Work Cultures

Start with your volunteer ERGs. Even though I pointed out their limitations earlier, ERGs can have substantial benefits. After all, an ERG is a group of folks at your company who share one important and valuable goal: creating a more inclusive workplace.

There can be ERGs for employees of color, LGBTQ+ employees, ERGs for women+ and allies—anything your particular company needs. If there isn't an ERG aligned with your goals, start one! People must feel safe to share in an ERG, so these are usually employee-run. Sure, you can include managers (or allies!) of your named affinity, but if the problem is workplace toxicity, and you think having a manager there might keep people silent, take your group offline and offsite to keep people's trust.

Get organized. From your ERGs, you can grow a company-wide inclusion effort. Executive leadership can and should be involved and can help gain buy-in from other leaders; this is another place where allyship training pays off. But be clear: ERGs must inform leadership with their findings. It should not have to do the inclusion work for the entire company but rather have a strong and respected voice at the highest levels to be effective. As an example, here's how I like to structure effective ERGs:

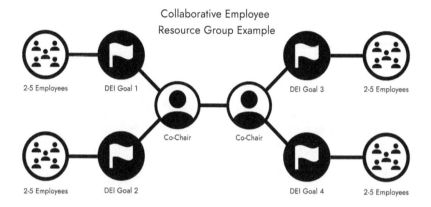

Collaborative Employee
Resource Group Example

2-5 Employees   DEI Goal 1   Co-Chair   Co-Chair   DEI Goal 3   2-5 Employees

2-5 Employees   DEI Goal 2   DEI Goal 4   2-5 Employees

#blackintheivory

If you want to know the state of DEI in academia, just take a look at this string of tweets posted with the hashtag #blackintheivory.

"Having a white male patient say, 'I would have been a doctor, but they didn't accept me because they started handing out medical school admissions to black women instead' while your white male attending nods in agreement."

"Was told by one of my former best friends that the 'only reason I got into #Harvard med was that I was Black.' So every time I struggled to memorize a metabolic pathway, every time I didn't get the grade, every time I was talked over in class...I heard her voice."

"Said to me by white male attendings at a med school interview: 'I just don't see you becoming a surgeon.' At a residency interview: 'Surgery has historically been made up of white males...so how do you think you'll fit in here?' Make room."

"#BlackintheIvory is being admitted to a grad program only to be met with surprise by the faculty member who agreed over email to be your advisor. By surprise, I mean they expressed shock at the fact that I was Black when I walked in the room during the prospective student visit."

"In HS: 'U only got into Penn bc ur Black'

In College: 'U only got into that master's program bc ur Black'

In Grad: 'U only got into that master's program bc ur Black'

In Grad: 'U only got into med school w/ur numbers bc ur Black'"

Another reason such blatant, unexamined racism is so disheartening in academia (apart from the obvious shown above), is the fact that we regularly hear arguments about how we no longer need affirmative action, and that can impact policies that promote diversity in universities and places of higher learning. Academia is one of the most racist and sexist institutions due to the entirely misguided belief that only "uneducated" individuals can be racist.[68]

As Ijeoma Oluo explains in her book *So You Want to Talk about Race*: "Affirmative action is a critical tool if we want to mitigate some of the effects of systemic racism and misogyny in our society. It should not be rolled back; in fact, I argue that it should be expanded to other groups that suffer from systemic oppression as well. Moreover, when affirmative action is viewed as 'enough,' it can be detrimental to the fight for racial justice. We must never forget that without systemic change and without efforts to battle the myriad of ways in which systemic racism impacts people of color in all classes, backgrounds and abilities, our efforts at ending systemic racial oppression will fail.[69]"

In one of my interviews, I discussed the issue of racist systems in institutions of higher learning with a woman (we'll call her Alyssa) who was a PhD candidate at the time studying at Georgia Tech in a very prestigious program. The university she had come from for undergrad had a lot of diversity, and there was a program in place for students to get to know each other and make friends, especially those from underrepresented groups as she is. She's now a professor at the University

---

68   Robin DiAngelo, *White Fragility: Why It's so Hard for White People to Talk about Racism* (Boston: Beacon Press, 2018).

69   Ijeoma Oluo, *So You Want to Talk about Race.* (New York: Seal Press, 2019).

of Florida. But when she started in this new program at Georgia Tech, things were very different.

"I remember my PI sitting me down ahead of my advisory meeting and saying, 'If any of their questions seem wrong to you, or unfair to you, I want you to tell me,'" said Alyssa. "He was also Black, and gay, so he was very proactive when it came to his mentees being treated fairly. I thought, *How can anything the advisors say be wrong, and how am I to judge it? They are some of the most brilliant minds in our field, and I'm just me.* But when I sat down with the committee, I realized what he'd meant. When white students flubbed an answer, it was assumed that they possessed the requisite knowledge but that they just had misunderstood the question, and the committee was lenient. If I messed up an answer, they thought I'd gotten into the program because of affirmative action and didn't belong there at all. Or that I'd 'taken' a spot from a more deserving white student. I had to work twice as hard to prove that wasn't the case. Both to them and myself."

Removing affirmative action policies immediately leads to a drop off in URGs being represented at schools. This immediately impacts diversity in the workforce because many of these schools operate as "feeders" to big tech, start-ups, and STEM companies. These companies believe that universities and colleges are doing the work of promoting the "best" of URGs, and in reality, they are doing marginally better than nothing.

Furthermore, despite the claims that women+ and people of color no longer need affirmative action or that affirmative action initiatives discriminate against white men, evidence demonstrates that discrimination against white men is rare. For example, of the 91,000 employment discrimination cases before the Equal Employment Opportunity Commission, approximately 3% are discrimination cases against white men. Further, a study conducted by Rutgers University and commissioned by the U.S. Department of Labor (1995) found that discrimination against white men is not a significant problem in employment and that a "high proportion" of claims brought by white men are "*without merit.*"[70]

TL;DR:

- Psychological safety is the number one predictor of success in the workplace.
- For DEI (Diversity, Equity, and Inclusion. Remember?), this means examining your current teams. Are they inclusive? If a candidate walks into your office, are they seeing themselves represented? Are they talking to employees who can answer their questions about how someone like them can expect to be treated? Do you have nongendered bathrooms?
- ERGs are a good starting point, but they only work if the buck doesn't stop with the group. Senior leaders need information to address noninclusive practices happening under their watch.

70   Upstate Medical University, "Affirmative Action: Myth versus Reality | Diversity and Inclusion," www.upstate.edu, accessed January 26, 2021, https://www.upstate.edu/diversityinclusion/policies-and-procedures/aa/myth_reality.php.

Chapter 4

BUILDING COMMUNITIES
FOR SOCIAL JUSTICE

When I was a kid, I thought only Tupac Shakur understood me. That might be weird to hear given how I look now, but when I was growing up in poverty, songs that I was hearing on the radio just weren't speaking to my experience. I was coming up in a place where most people were living lives with their basic needs met—where people grew up in the sunshine with their parents and their siblings. We couldn't relate to each other. I stuck out. Kids, and even their parents, treated me badly. Teachers were awful to me and often hated me for reasons I attributed to my worth. I was on free lunch, and for whatever reason, this gave other kids the message that my parents didn't care enough about me to pay for me to eat.

Parents weren't doing a good job raising inclusive kids, at least when I was a kid. Maybe we still aren't. But when Tupac sang about being on food stamps; family members being missing from you; and feeling like no one saw the pain it caused to be so invisible that people didn't even know about the kind of life you could be living, being made worse by the world thinking you deserved it—I felt seen. In Tupac's words, "Tupac cares, if don't nobody else care."[71]

When I was 14, I was still struggling to fit in as a freshman in a largely privileged school; I was an outlier. In a desperate attempt to force a conversation about what was happening to me, I wrote a 10-page paper for American History class on how Tupac was a poet. I broke down all of his lyrics and tied them back to their historical context. That's how long this has been my fight—my receipts go back 20 years. So when I take to social media to talk to people about social justice, it isn't because it's trending. It's because I've always been here. I assumed that teaching history in the context of the social justice fights we were seeing every day would be a good use case. I was right and wrong.

Building a Community for Allyship

In May 2020, I created a Facebook group intended to be a safe place for teaching allyship. At its inception, I intended for the "Ally Up!" group to be an educational space to include mini educational videos (by me) for what I called "bite-sized historical context." I promised educational videos, history, book recommendations, and articles that talked about the topics I was covering and more. Further, I promised that the group would be learning from me (and each other) about structural racism and other oppressive systems in America. I wanted it to be a community that valued each voice wherever they were in their journey to support people who wanted to be better allies.

Weaponizing Whiteness

I launched the group earlier than I had intended when Amy Cooper and Christian Cooper (no relation) ran into each other in The Bramble of New York City's Central Park. Ms. Cooper, a white woman, was

---

71   "Keep Ya Head Up" is a 1993 hit single by Tupac Shakur. The song features R&B singer Dave Hollister and is dedicated to Black women and Latasha Harlins.

walking her adopted dog without a leash when Mr. Cooper, an avid bird-watcher and a Black man, stepped forward. Mr. Cooper asked Ms. Cooper to put her dog on a leash, as the posted signage indicated was the law. She refused. He insisted politely from a safe distance. She apparently became enraged and threatened to call the police and tell them "an African American man was threatening [her] life."

We can only assume she expected Mr. Cooper to understand her threat through a shared cultural awareness (and coded language) that the police have historically, and up to this writing, been infamously and statistically more violent with Black people—particularly Black men.[72] The fact that they both knew this is crucial to understanding what played out next in society and on social media. Mr. Cooper, upon hearing this, took out his phone and began recording their interaction. This escalated the situation, at least in Ms. Cooper's mind, and she in fact did call the police. We watch via Mr. Cooper's video from a safe distance where Ms. Cooper playacts being scared by raising her pitch, pacing, and repeating that "an African American, a Black man" was threatening her life. Ms. Cooper understood that she was weaponizing her whiteness; she knew what the police would do even if she didn't completely understand the why. Even if she didn't understand academically from culture, history, or society how exactly this was possible, she did know how to use her whiteness to make herself a threat to this man.

When this became news, Black people and people who know their history found this story to be horribly familiar to the more tragic story of Emmett Till, who was murdered by a gang of white men in Mississippi in 1955 for allegedly whistling at a white woman in a store. The white woman, Carolyn Bryant, was the wife of the store's proprietor and told

72 Annalisa Merelli, "Black People Are at the Center of Two Public Health Crises in the US: Covid-19 and Police Brutality," *Quartz*, May 31, 2020, https://qz.com/1862403/black-people-are-at-the-center-of-two-public-health-crises-in-the-us-covid-19-and-police-brutality/.

her husband upon his return from a business trip that the 14-year-old Till had "grabbed her, made lewd advances, and wolf-whistled at her on his way out."[73] Roy Bryant rounded up a posse, went to Till's uncle's house where Till was staying, and dragged Emmett Till away. These adult men stripped and beat the 14-year-old child nearly to death, gouged out his eyes, shot him in the head, and then threw his lifeless body into the river tied to a cotton-gin fan with barbed wire. Carolyn Bryant recanted her testimony 60 years after Till's murder.[74]

The outcome of the story with Amy Cooper and Christian Cooper was different because, and only because, Mr. Cooper had thought to record their interaction. Amy Cooper received the weight of the blame for the interaction and was rightly called a racist. She was publicly shamed, she lost her job, and the rescue asked for its dog back. As we all know, this could have gone much differently. When this story made the rounds on social media, I heard the outcries from white folks, especially women, which ranged from disbelief to full-on self-flagellation:

"I'm shocked."

"I can't believe this happened."

"I hate her."

"I'm so ashamed to be white." A few people even threatened harm to Ms. Cooper. Some people, on the other hand, suggested that we didn't know what had happened before the video had started recording. "Maybe she did feel threatened; does that make her a racist?"

Since so many of the comments were *at least* problematic, I decided I'd start the group early to educate on situations like this for the future. If white people could weaponize their privilege, my style of allyship where

---

73 History.com Editors, "Emmett Till Is Murdered," History, August 28, 2018, https://www.history.com/this-day-in-history/the-death-of-emmett-till.

74 Richard Pérez-Peña, "Woman Linked to 1955 Emmett Till Murder Tells Historian Her Claims Were False," *New York Times*, January 27, 2017, https://www.nytimes.com/2017/01/27/us/emmett-till-lynching-carolyn-bryant-donham.html.

privilege is used to help others would work too; teaching historical and social context with empathy could have an impact. I started building "Ally Up!" as a private group with some educational resources and invited no one.

Black Lives Matter

The next day, news broke that a Black man named George Floyd had been killed by a white police officer with three other officers present in Minnesota. An onlooker recorded the officer kneeling on Mr. Floyd's neck while he begged that he couldn't breathe, that his body hurt, and begged for his deceased mother. The nation watched in horror for more than eight minutes as the life drained from Mr. Floyd, murdered by an officer of the law. I posted a video about how to receive the grief and outrage from our friends and family of color and proceeded to add about 20 of my personal friends who I considered aspiring allies to the group.

The next morning, I woke up to find 89 aspiring allies studiously sharing information and content. I worked throughout the day to stay ahead of their questions; meet any awareness of structural racism and other systemic forms of oppression; and expand on that knowledge to turn them into the kind of allies who could advocate effectively. I confirmed over and over that the group was a place for aspiring allies to come with their questions and their lack of understanding to learn together and not be shamed. People were outraged by what had happened to George Floyd and wanted to be better. They could finally see the impact structural and systemic racism was having on the BIPOC community and wanted to know more.

People were asking questions; they were vulnerable about their lack of knowledge and they continued to add friends and loved ones. Most interestingly, when people saw friends and family of color who were hurting or outraged, they added them to the group. I was clear that the intent was not to use the emotional labor of BIPOC but to share the space for them to talk about their pain and outrage if they wished. Or they could just watch. We talked openly about white allyship versus white saviorism. We planned out a book club and which books would have the most impact on their allyship.

Protests broke out immediately across the nation. We talked about how to support protestors, where to donate to bail funds, how to protest safely, where protests were taking place, and how to participate. Riots and looting started happening at night; curfews began nationwide. We discussed the history of riots and how they have impacted change in the United States, citing the Boston Tea Party and Stonewall. Donald Trump cleared a street filled with peaceful protestors and a church where folks were gathering for medical attention and water with rubber bullets and tear gas; ultimately, we'd learn this was for a photo op. Everyone was outraged, including the church leaders.

People were coming to the group wanting to have answers to cite against propaganda posts about Martin Luther King Jr. and peaceful protests. We talked about how white people were just as angry about Colin Kaepernick kneeling silently in protest as they were about people marching in the streets; what did that tell us? How it seemed people were only comfortable with protests they could ignore. We discussed at length how divisive and hated Martin Luther King Jr. had been in his time, so much so that he had been assassinated. As talks continued to get more authentic, more and more people were added. We were not even a week into this invite-only group, and we had almost 600 participants learning about allyship.

Confronting Law Enforcement

One night, to my great surprise, a police officer was added by a friend of his to the group. The officer was agitated but respectful. He posed questions about the complicated issues facing law enforcement and asked the community for input. Each person who started an interaction with him came in hot. We'd all seen terrible miscarriages of justice by police against citizens for days, and here he was. On the inside, I was panicking. I thought, *This is the end, it was great while it lasted.* But I was wrong. He was direct, he knew why he was there, he knew the issues, and he wanted to help confront them on the ground. By the end, around 30 comment thread participants, including me, were thanking him for his honest participation. He eventually left, offended by the antipolice feelings shared in the group. On the one hand, it seemed like he was honestly interested, and on the other, it seemed like he couldn't handle the blowback of what his brothers and sisters in law enforcement were being recorded doing every day, without being seen as an individual and not responsible for his group. I would note the irony of that, but I'm sure it would have been lost on him. Handing out allyship cookies wasn't really the group's thing.

Building Your Own Allyship Group

Multiple people and organizations have approached me from everywhere in the country asking about the "right way" to build a group for promoting allyship. While there are no definitive rules to build a "perfect" group, I've dedicated the remainder of this chapter to capture a set of basic guidelines and lessons we learned along the way. Many of your white group members will be encountering the concept of systemic racism (and their place in it) for the first time, and it's important to build a safe place for people to share and work through their feelings, or else you'll find your community flying off the rails.

With this in mind, here are the posted moderator rules for the "Ally Up!" group:

- Employ a vouching system: You may add friends who are aspiring allies, but you are responsible for them.

- Reinforce the fact that everyone has bias: We freely admit this, own it, and recognize that we're here to grow and learn to do better.
- Trust, and do better: If you're here, you clearly want to do better. If someone has invited you, they trust you want to do better. Racism, homophobia, transphobia, misogyny, xenophobia, etc. are not tolerated.
- Read before commenting.
- No hate speech or bullying.
- Respect and protect everyone's privacy.
- No spam.
- This group is a place for a diversity of ideas, not a diversity of morals.

Lesson 1: What Right Do You Have?

As members were appearing faster than I could count and posts were going up faster than we could tag topics or flag them for review, I started getting direct messages (DMs) entirely from white folks demanding to know why this group existed, what right I had to lead it, what my qualifications were, and why they should learn anything from me. People's first messages to me were to comment about how wrong I am about everything. Did I have an agenda? What was it? You can't say "ally." You have to say "aspiring ally." You can't say "ally." You have to say "conspirator."[75] You can't call *yourself* an ally. The messages were piling up.

I eventually recorded and released a video to talk about who I am, what my social justice experience is, what my professional experience is, and what my lived experience is. I explained that I knew it was jarring to "wake up" in a system of racism. I knew how they felt. But I pleaded

---

75 "Module 13: Allies & Antiracism," Project READY, accessed January 26, 2021, https://ready.web.unc.edu/section-1-foundations/module-13-allies-antiracism/.

with them to sit in those feelings and work on the guilt, the shame, and the anger, and not just redirect them onto me. I was probably too vulnerable and too authentic, but I've only had to do it once, and I eventually stopped receiving messages.

So when creating your own group, you need to recognize that people are going to come at you from all levels of understanding. You aren't going to be the expert; you don't really need to be. What you do need to be is willing to be a lifelong learner with an ability to center[76] the conversation on the people affected by the issue and a willingness to yield the floor. Be authentic, be humble, and fail forward.

Lesson 2: The Becky

June 1st rolled in, and we were in the thick of the Black Lives Matter protests. June 1st is also when Pride starts to commemorate the Stonewall Riots.[77] One of my gay family[78] members posted in the group how important the riots were, how the LGBTQ+ community was standing with Black Lives Matter and was dedicating all Pride events to BLM. A member commented immediately: "Posts like these aren't helpful, and you need to educate yourself!"

My family member texted me: "I'm already done with this allyship group. I tagged you."

I checked my phone and read the interaction 10 times before I realized: Becky never read the post! (Becky isn't her real name). I asked

---

76 Centering something is to take the person affected as the focal point (as opposed to yourself) and add the context of their lived experience and histories to the issue rather than your own. For example, saying "as a white person…" is centering yourself.

77 History.com Editors, "Stonewall Riots," History, June 26, 2020, https://www. history.com/topics/gay-rights/the-stonewall-riots.

78 Family: capital F Family is how people in the LGBTQ+ community refer to each other. For example, instead of asking me if I'm queer, another member would say "are you Family?" The person I'm referring to here is actually a part of my adopted family as well; he's uncle to my children.

her if she could be more specific about what about the post wasn't helpful to BLM, and she instead doubled down. She eventually admitted she didn't read his post but insisted that he should educate himself more to be helpful. Someone much calmer than I popped in and posted, "Hey, Becky, there are Black people in the LGBTQ+ community. Hope that helps." Mic drop. Excellent.

I'm not sure what happened to Becky. I haven't seen her around. But my gay family member stayed and felt supported by the group, and that mattered to me.

Lesson 3: The Chad

Our next allyship test came when Chad (not his real name) was added to the group. He joined with a controversial message announcing his arrival: "I've been asked to join this group to give a real-world perspective on the issues." Fine. He's white, wearing sunglasses, and sitting in his car in his profile picture. He goes on to note that he has no problem with anyone and doesn't care if people are gay "as long as a couple of gay guys don't rape [him] in an alley." Here we go.

Almost immediately, people asked him to remove the parts of his post that were offensive to those who identify as members of the LGBTQ+ community. I welcomed him to the group and let him know that his post was offensive and that he needed to remove it. He thanked me but refused to edit the post because he "stands by it." The next day, he posted a racist comment about "Uncle Toms."[79] Chad started inciting more arguments with people, defending his right to post what he wanted as long as he's learning.

Chad felt that posting offensive and racially charged comments was his way of fulfilling the role of devil's advocate. Now, in my extensive

---

79 "Uncle Tom" is an expression that describes a Black person who is overly eager to please and impress white folks; it comes from the book *Uncle Tom's Cabin* by Harriet Beecher Stowe.

experience discussing racism with literally every type of human of age, we hear the term "devil's advocate" when someone wants to be racist, knows they're probably being racist, and doesn't want to be called out for it. One of my dearest Black mentors when I was living in Atlanta liked to say that "The devil is all around, doing just fine. He doesn't need advocates." Ultimately, we had to say bye to Chad and removed him from the group.

People like Chad are here to teach us a very valuable lesson— some people are *just now* coming to the realization that there are some spaces not designed exclusively for their comfort. This usually triggers an array of responses from anger to some serious mental gymnastics about their intentions, and how you as the group leader have to make accommodations for their learning and prioritize their needs over everyone else's. As someone who was raised in literally the opposite scenario, I have found myself thinking, *Well, that must be nice.*

Lesson 4: Drama for Drama's Sake

By this point, new members were appearing by the hundreds, and I continued to add trusted friends of mine of all ethnicities[80] with very different backgrounds and lived experiences to help me moderate. Things continued to deteriorate outside in the world. People were protesting, and videos were being shared hourly of police overreach and abuse. I watched them all, and shockingly, comments were surprisingly cordial between members. People really wanted to talk to their loved ones about what was going on and declare their support for racial justice. They wanted to find out more about how to advance progress and whom to call. A PhD genius friend of mine in the group volunteered to lead the "Square One Book Club" so members could read books together and educate themselves rather than leaning on people of color in our lives

---

80 And "races."

to teach us about racism. Most surprising was the number of people of color dropping in to thank us for being there. Everyone was cool about it. Everyone knew we weren't there for "allyship cookies."

At one point, someone from my city shared a post from a local police officer friend of hers. He mused how ridiculous it was that our city was "allowing" people to attend a Black Lives Matter protest yet wasn't allowing any Fourth of July events. "Should be an interesting 4th!" he said. She asked the group how she should discuss it with him. I quoted our mayor on the issue and watched to make sure the responses were thoughtful and thought nothing else of it.

The next day, she posted again in the group that someone who knew them both had taken a screenshot of her post and reported it to him. Obviously, this was a rule violation of the group. She went on to demand the person who shared it reveal themselves and upped the ante by telling people she was scared for her life now that the group had been reported to the police. I reached out to her directly, and she revealed that she and the officer were not at odds; she had decided to weaponize her (female) whiteness to force a confession about the screenshot from someone she knew in the group.

A handful of members messaged me and told me they were scared to be involved if the local police were going to hurt them for participating in the group. Suddenly, members started leaving. One member even called me and the other moderators out for not protecting the "victim." For the sake of transparency, I announced to the group what happened, apologized that a member had broken the rules of the group, and reminded them that there is no functionality in Facebook that would prevent anyone from screenshotting a post in a private group and sharing it. Some people "liked" the post, and a few more members decided to leave. The rest of the members seemed satisfied.

At that point, I reached back out to the original poster, asking to be put in touch with the officer so I might discuss his feelings on the matter as a representative of the group. She told me he "doesn't see a direct threat from [our] little secret group at this time."

I reminded her that the group isn't secret; it's private so it doesn't become a free-for-all, but that doesn't mean we want to exclude him or anyone else. I assume he declined my invitation because I didn't hear from the officer or the poster again.

So the lesson here is people come to social media for drama, and that reality will exist for you no matter how serious the intent of your endeavor is. People are people.

Lesson 5: The Not-Devil's Advocate

Later, someone I know from a professional networking group joined the Facebook group and asked how to talk to members of her family that weren't keen on the antipolice conversation taking place around the country. Some of them were in law enforcement. Many members offered helpful suggestions and heartfelt support, except for one particularly vocal member of the group—our self-proclaimed "Not-Devil's Advocate."[81] Instead of offering support, he attempted to shame her for her "white supremacist" family and her ability to only now see them for what they are. One of our moderators rightly decided to delete his comment, and I backed his play. There's no room for hate in our group. The Not-Devil's Advocate did not take this well.

He decided to message me directly and demand that I find out who deleted his post, accused me of tone policing, and called me a coward. With a stern and direct response, I explained my position, reminded him of the rules, and warned him to be respectful in all manner of discourse. He thanked me for my candor and told me he hoped we could be friends. As it turns out, this won't be the last conversation we'll have about his approach.

---

81 This person instead demanded I recognize him as a "chaos agent." I disagreed.

The lesson is that taking the "devil's advocate" position in this context is white-centered privilege masquerading as concern for the integrity of the argument. In a conversation about "race" or white supremacy, not all sides of the argument are equally valid and deserving of equal attention.

Lesson 6: Support People of Color

One day, a Black member of the group—let's call him Mike—added a photo of light-skinned synchronized swimmers performing in support of Black Lives Matter wearing African-print swimsuits with swim caps displaying a cornrow-like pattern. His comment expressed his disapproval, and the majority of the group rightly noted the accidental racism on display. One white member of the group—let's call him Aidan—demanded to know why this photo was racist. Mike politely explained that cornrows came from a tradition of weaving escape routes into hair to help slaves run to freedom. Still, Aidan refused to understand. He retorted that anyone who didn't answer him nicely could F off and underlined his point with a middle-finger emoji.[82]

A storm of comments was flying back and forth, and the moderators struggled to keep up with the reports on Aidan's comments. Aidan wanted to know why it wasn't racist for women of color to straighten their hair. I regretted that a person of color felt that they had to do the emotional work of explaining to Aidan why his comments were racist, but we couldn't get ahead of everything that was happening. Ultimately, the moderators decided that it was right to delete the reported posts and ban Aidan from the group.

Deleting the posts sparked controversy with our resident Not-Devil's Advocate—he felt that Tom, the moderator who was removing the posts, was unjustified in removing the offending comments. At this point, Not-Devil's Advocate took a more direct approach, starting a new

---

82 That is tone policing.

thread and tagging Tom, who is a person of color, demanding he be "removed from power." In speaking to Tom, who was just doing his job, he noted that "It's fine, just another white guy looking down on me and assuming I don't know what I'm doing, like every other day."

I stepped in, trying to keep even while I felt rage building. I told the mod I would handle the situation. I tagged Not-Devil's Advocate and demanded he apologize to the mod immediately for this behavior. He ignored me and continued to double down about how wrong it is to delete posts. I explained that we decided as a group that racist posts that were hurtful to people of color should be removed so as not to further hurt people of color who would read them. We went back and forth for over an hour in public threads while he tried every argument he could think of to center himself as the aggrieved party. He insisted that it was better to leave the racist comments up so he could learn.

He never learned anything. He was never moved. But I kept going anyway.

So what's the lesson? Why did I waste my time on Not-Devil's Advocate knowing he'd never be moved? Because he wasn't the only one watching the conversation. More than 900 people in the group watched me repeatedly hold him accountable while he tried over and over to redirect, deflect, and assure me that Tom's *ethnicity didn't matter and he'd have said the same thing to a white guy.* Eventually, I put Not-Devil's Advocate on probation for a month and removed the threads as they had served their purpose in the moment. It was important to me that Tom (and the rest of the group) saw that I would defend him to the hilt and defend people of color who were working hard for free to help educate allies, even if ultimately this one white guy was immovable.

People of Color Demand Allyship

Nearly one month after the group was formed, people of color began asking to add friends and family who still harbored racist views and continued to defend white supremacist talking points. I was curious; that was not something I had anticipated. I had figured eventually the right thing to do would be to make the group more public. I hadn't considered that people of color would basically be asking us to put our money where our mouths were and take on the burden of educating people that matter to them who were racist.

From my perspective, I believe that eliminating racism through education, empathy, and action is entirely the responsibility of white aspiring allies. I have said many times only white people benefit from racism the same way that only men benefit from the patriarchy. If we want these things to change, it must be the people who benefit from these systems taking on the lion's share of the burden of changing them. We must take on the responsibility of self-education, of talking to the people most affected and demanding change within our home, work, and social communities. What we are currently working on is the best way to protect members and expand into educating people who don't already understand there's work that needs to be done. At least when it comes to social networking, safe spaces and public spaces seem to be mutually exclusive.

TL;DR:

- Social media, in my now-extensive experience, is the second hardest place to teach social justice issues. The first is in the workplace.
- I started a Facebook group as an extension of the DEI work I was doing, and people came in and fought with me in real time as they found themselves "waking up" in systemic racism for the first time and wanting someone to blame.
- Let your diverse team members lead on these issues, and support them with all the passion in your heart.

- Self-education is absolutely critical to allyship and effective advocacy.
- Political values have less to do with who supported social justice initiatives in the group than my biases had assumed, not entirely, but less than I thought.
- If you even lightly suggest people examine their own biases when they use racist or misogynistic tropes to talk about people they don't like who share those identities, you will get flamed like crazy.
- People who had been added by others who thought they cared about social justice attacked me personally regularly, which is why people with less power sometimes let things go in high-risk situations such as work.
- Even people who call themselves allies have work to do on their self-education and social justice understanding.

PART 2

HIRING WITH INCLUSIVITY

It's 1990. I'm seven years old, and my foster mother is hurling slurs about every stereotype imaginable. She's an angry, spiteful woman who looks like the mom on *Everybody Loves Raymond*, but acts like Lyssa, the Greek goddess of rage, fury, and crazed frenzy.

She abuses me. She calls me a mutt. (My birth father is a brown-skinned Hispanic man, and my mother is Irish—as far as I know.) I'm trapped not only in the broken foster care system but also, more importantly, struggling with a nebulous identity wrapped up in race. I escape through reading; by high school, I'm best friends with the librarian, who's asking me about my recommendations for the next great book. Through obsessive reading, I'm learning this isn't normal. This doesn't have to be it for me.

And then, my "mother" kicks me out as soon as I age out of the foster care system, no longer bringing her money from the State of Massachusetts. I'm homeless with $650 to my name and a laundry basket filled with all my worldly possessions.

Today, whenever I talk about diversity and inclusion—and let me be clear, it seems to be absolutely crucial for people to decide if I have any idea what I'm talking about or if I have any right to say it—I often ask a group I'm speaking to who and what they think my identities are.

51

I get all kinds of guesses. They glance at my face, my eyes, my skin, my shape, my ring finger, and they usually conclude: Straight white woman. Actually, I'm not just white; I'm also half Hispanic. But if I don't tell people, then no one knows. I walk a fine line with both identities: wanting to own my white privilege that I benefit from, and wanting to share my Hispanic identity as well. I'm also not straight. I'm a queer cisgendered woman. This doesn't mean I didn't struggle; obviously, it just means my skin wasn't one of the things making life harder. That's the definition of white privilege.

But that's not even the issue: who can speak about racism? And when, and with what authority, is white supremacist thinking keeping oppressed people oppressed. Trust me: oppressed groups have been fighting for their human rights for generations, and if they had the power to free themselves, they already would have. They don't, and we know that. People who benefit from these systems—you, me, your coworkers—need to do the work to dismantle racism, sexism, homophobia, transphobia, and others in our workforces because our voices are louder by the nature of these systems of inequity. We are the ones who benefit from them, and if I can share that load, so can you. You don't have to know everything; you just need to start making it a priority to understand and learn. To continue your education in allyship, you need to surround yourself with diverse teams, allow them equity in their career endeavors, and support their growth with inclusive policies and practices on the job.

Chapter 5
ATTRACTING THE RIGHT CANDIDATES

The quickest way to show you're prioritizing DEI in your company is to stand out from the crowd.[83] This means refreshing your hiring funnel strategy because it's often a candidate's first glimpse into your hiring and work culture.

So why are so many job descriptions so hostile and arbitrary? Long bulleted lists of buzzwords, skill requirements, and obtuse language that filters people out instead of in—nope. Candidates almost always get their first impression of your hiring and work culture by reading your job descriptions, which you can improve by following these 10 guidelines:[84]

1. Be welcoming.

Job descriptions should be an invitation to join your team, so make sure you describe the hiring team's goals and the company's overall

---

83 Di Ciruolo, "10 Changes You Can Make Right Now to Improve Diversity in Your Hiring Funnel (Especially in Tech)," Medium, January 3, 2020, https://medium.com/swlh/10-changes-you-can-make-right-now-to-improve-diversity-in-your-hiring-funnel-especially-in-tech-b183208701f3.

84 Ciruolo, "Improve Diversity in Your Hiring Funnel (Especially in Tech)."

mission well enough that candidates can imagine themselves joining. Even better, list some examples of how someone who joins the team will make a positive impact, particularly if there's a skill you're desperately in need of to round out your team. Some examples of welcoming language include: "You'll find a good fit here if you love…" or "Our team is looking for someone to help us with…" or even, "We'd love to hear your ideas about how we can improve…" Ultimately, you want to entice candidates to learn more about you and imagine themselves already a part of your team, not discourage them with a laundry list of arbitrary requirements.

2. Be genuine.

Slow down on hyperbolic adjectives in your job invitations such as, "Join an insanely innovative team!" Instead of aggressive and grandiose generalities, channel your excitement into a passionate description of the company and the team—tell your candidates why you're excited to work where you do. Hyperbolic statements intending to drum up excitement in your audience typically have the opposite effect. Also no one is fooling anyone with that "diversity of thought"[85] line. Please stop. It's cringetastic. It's like a bedazzled banner that says: *We don't get it!*

3. Be aware.

Without realizing it, your job description is likely using language from your affinity group that can tell the reader who you are as a writer. Many job descriptions are plagued by this "coded language" that often

---

85   Rebekah Bastian, "Why We Need to Stop Talking about Diversity of Thought," *Forbes*, May 13, 2019, https://www.forbes.com/sites/rebekahbastian/2019/05/13/why-we-need-to-stop-talking-about-diversity-of-thought/#6d49695a67c3. Diversity of thought is a term being used to say that just because a company or team all looks the same, doesn't mean they don't bring different innovative ideas to the table. And it's not being used for the most part to be more inclusive to folks who aren't neurotypical.

prevents candidates from applying at all. It takes practice and self-reflection to get better at improving your writing voice, but it will serve you well in many other endeavors beyond your hiring funnel. If you're looking to attract a broader candidacy, a great way to start is to have as many team members as possible review your job description before posting it. I've spent a long time helping others edit and develop an inclusive writing style and tone, so if you have any doubts, check out Textio or others—there's an answer for this.

4. Be clear.

Make sure you know what skills you really need before adding them to your openings. Make a list of "must-haves" versus "nice-to-haves," or, better yet, describe the tech stack in both historical and aspirational terms. What kind of impact will a successful candidate have, and how is impact on the team assessed and rewarded? A senior engineer may not have expert knowledge of your legacy technologies, but they may be an expert in a technology you're trying to move to. Adding every programming language under the sun to your list of "must-haves" not only drives down diversity it also reflects poorly on you as an organization to not be able to hire for realistic roles with relevant skills. Even worse, 40% of women will not apply to jobs if they feel they don't have every requirement completely checked.[86]

On the engineering side, make sure to let senior candidates know you're flexible about specific languages too—if you're looking for someone who's an expert in microservices but doesn't necessarily have expertise in the platform or language you use, they could still be a great fit if they're interested in learning something new and bringing their experience to your team. Passionate engineers learn on and off the job,

---

86 Tara Sophia Mohr, "Why Women Don't Apply for Jobs Unless They're 100% Qualified," *Harvard Business Review*, August 25, 2014, https://hbr.org/2014/08/why-women-dont-apply-for-jobs-unless-theyre-100-qualified.

and many skills (especially programming languages and design patterns) are transferable. Make sure to plan for your teammates' career growth accordingly.

5. Be flexible.

If you're looking for a senior individual contributor role, you should absolutely consider developing a remote work policy if you don't already have one. Many of the people I talk to with any seniority have reached a point in their career where they care about the flexibility to work remotely for a majority of the time rather than being placed into an ill-fitting, on-site mentor or manager role. If you do have a remote work policy, it's essential to have it noted in your job description—senior candidates will include it in their search terms and filter you out if you don't.

6. Be mindful.

For non-entry-level positions, expand your description to include the previous level of experience. For example, if you're looking for a senior software engineer, try "mid-senior software engineer" for the title. Or, even better, remove specific titles such as "senior" or "lead," and allow the description itself to outline the kinds of help you're looking for. You'll find you've widened your candidacy net by a mile, and you'll be surprised to find even more applicants who fit your requirements applying. Many candidates are looking for new gigs because they're stagnating at their existing jobs and don't even realize their skills have progressed to the level that you're looking for. Certain affinities of people (especially those coming from toxic work environments) do not consider themselves "senior" or feel hesitant about whether or not you would consider them "senior." Every individual will have a range of different skills and focus on how they're growing in their career, so be flexible with titles and responsibilities, and use your interview process to determine skill level and aptitude to place them at an appropriate level to succeed.

7. Be inclusive.

Stop putting barriers up that reduce the number of places you receive candidates from. By only looking in one place (like only working with "feeder" schools) or only looking for folks with a specific length of experience (10+ years of SQL? Honey, please.), you're obviously going to drive down diversity. Here are a few examples I've seen in the wild:

- Requiring unnecessary degrees or experience
- Recruiting only from Ivy League universities
- Excluding folks with nontraditional career paths
- Poor performance on unrelated standardized tests

Remember, standardization in the hiring process disproportionately penalizes women and people of color. Don't fall into the trap of letting past performers dictate your hiring strategy forever, or you'll end up with a lot of the same people solving problems in the exact same way without any new perspectives or innovation.

8. Be involved.

Hiring managers and recruiters, by and large, are both guilty of excluding good candidates for bad reasons. Imagine a female recruiter at a tech conference telling a female software engineer with a disability to hide it from the hiring managers if she wants to get a job—true story! Avoid behaviors that don't support your values as a company. If you're hiring through a recruiter, be clear that you won't be interviewing anyone until you have a diverse pool of candidates to choose from. If you're dealing with an internal hiring manager, set annual diversity goals for the company, and tie a bonus to hitting those milestones.

9. Be smart.

Don't use standardized technical coding tests that someone on your senior team didn't have a hand in creating. If you don't have a senior team, or you don't know how to create your own strategy that tests the things you are actually looking for—there are companies that help you with that too. I recently had a candidate solve a problem in the complete opposite way the team thought we wanted, but because we knew what we were looking for as a team, we knew that she would be a huge asset to the company I was hiring for. Artificial intelligence testing solutions might be cheaper, but the technology just isn't developed enough to intuitively handle humans and all our infinite complexities just yet. Standardization and repeated results are what AI is built on, and we already know they are the enemy of diversity.

10. Be brave.

If your candidate pool consists of only one type of person, be brave enough to mention it to your team as a problem and come together to create solutions for it. Use the data! The most untapped source of diversity knowledge within a company is entry to mid-level, so talk to your staff and support them with need-based tools and resources to make better decisions moving forward.

URGs and Leadership

You need to have URGs on your C-Team. Full stop. Not *just* one role as chief of diversity. That's tokenism, and it's obvious. So if you want diverse candidates (and you do), you need to put your money where your mouth is. If you don't have URGs in leadership, savvy candidates—the ones you want—*will screen you out*. So you'll need to do the work and reach out directly to the people you want. It will be an uphill battle; other people are seeking those candidates as well. When they check out your all-white male leadership team, they likely aren't even going to respond to your emails. Don't get discouraged. Some will. And when they ask about your leadership, and you have to say you're all white guys, have a plan ready to change it. **Don't** just say, "You can be the first!" because women+ and other URG candidates have heard that before. You need to have a real, clear plan for how you are committed to changing the approach—*that's* how you stand out. And you will see it pay off.

AI and Hiring

I get asked a lot about the impact of AI on hiring. Actually, I get asked a lot about which programs people should be using and so far, I'm saying: I don't love anything I've seen yet, but let me tell you why. We all like to think of AI—and tech as a whole, really—as being neutral, having no biases or "isms" that would make it discriminatory. But that's not really true. As Safiya Umoja Noble explains in her book *Algorithms of Oppression*, it's the opposite. For example, if you were to google (as of this writing) "professional men's hairstyles," the search would return images entirely of white men. If you were to search for "unprofessional men's hairstyles," the first results you get back are Black men, with dreads and/or natural Black hair. That has an impact with real, negative consequences.

Consider an unsavvy HR person writing policy into a company effectively banning natural Black hair. A lot of us using Google think that these must just be the most popular results for our search. But Google is a business, not a library; it doesn't provide context. As Noble implores, "Now, more than ever, we need experts in the social sciences and digital humanities to engage in dialogue with activists and organizers, engineers, designers, information technologists, and public-policy makers before blunt artificial-intelligence decision-making trumps nuanced human decision-making."[87] She further notes, "We have to ask what is lost, who is harmed, and what should be forgotten with the embrace of artificial intelligence in decision-making."

I've had hundreds of interviews with women+ and URGs in tech and STEM fields, and one of the themes I hear is people being nervous about changing jobs, even when trying to escape toxic environments, because they need to consistently rewrite their resumes to "beat the AI." What? Is that what we wanted? The fact that the AI is slanting against nonwhite, nonmale candidates isn't news—especially to the talent we say we want. And the fact that women+ and minorities are underrepresented in tech isn't news either. Yet we keep trying the same thing and hoping it yields different outcomes. Or we convince ourselves that the AI is inclusive and is just weeding out unqualified candidates. What does "qualified" mean in this field? Seriously. I'm asking. Bill Gates, Steve Jobs, and Mark Zuckerberg all dropped out of college, so a college degree isn't the standard; we can agree there. Is it *which* college they dropped out of? In that case, are we leaving diversity and inclusion to colleges? We know how that goes.

How about this? John Doerr, a partner at venture capital firm Kleiner Perkins, said the following at the National Venture Capital Association's annual meeting: "In the early days, when you went in the back of Amazon's shipping area, the books were lined up. So you can see what people were buying. Invariably, there was a book about a programming language like Java. And in the same sales order, there was a book like *The Joy of Sex*. These [customers] were probably very clearly male nerds who had no social or sex lives trying to get help by using an online service. That correlates more with any other success factor that I've seen in the world's greatest entrepreneurs. If you look at Bezos or Marc Andreessen or David Filo, the founders of Google, they all seem

---

87 Safiya Umoja Noble, *Algorithms of Oppression: How Search Engines Reinforce Racism* (New York: New York University Press, 2018).

to be white, male nerds who dropped out of Harvard or Stanford, and they absolutely have no social life. So when I see that pattern coming in, which was true of Google, it's very easy to decide to invest."[88]

It seems like the more you adhere to "that pattern," the fewer degrees and less experience you need to have. The further away from that fictive narrative of what tech "looks like" you are, the more degrees and experience you need to have to be considered "qualified." Let's follow that: If we have artificial intelligence making "screening" decisions for us before we hire for jobs, who is impacted the most? Who's hurt by us trying to save some time? I actually don't have to guess, because Amazon famously already tried this. In an article for *Slate* titled "Amazon Created a Hiring Tool Using A.I. It Immediately Started Discriminating Against Women,"[89] Jordan Weissmann reports that Amazon started the project in 2014 to mechanize its staffing pool by combing through the Internet for "worthwhile" candidates. Of course, that's not all it did.

As Weissmann relays, Reuters reported the following: "In effect, Amazon's system taught itself that male candidates were preferable. It penalized resumes that included the word 'women's,' as in 'women's chess club captain.' And it downgraded graduates of two all-women's colleges. The program also decided that basic tech skills, like the ability to write code, which popped up on all sorts of resumes, weren't all that important, but grew to like candidates who littered their resumes with macho verbs such as 'executed' and 'captured.'"

Basically, AI didn't remove biases, it *automated* them.

Amazon abandoned the project. "At a time when lots of companies are embracing artificial intelligence for things like hiring," Weissmann

---

88   Elissa Shevinsky, "Introduction," in *Lean Out: The Struggle for Gender Equality in Tech and Startup Culture*, ed. Elissa Shevinsky (New York: OR Books, 2015), 10.

89   Jordan Weissmann, "Amazon Created a Hiring Tool Using AI. It Immediately Started Discriminating against Women.," *Slate Magazine*, October 10, 2018, https://slate.com/business/2018/10/amazon-artificial-intelligence-hiring-discrimination-women.html.

concludes, "what happened at Amazon really highlights that using such technology without unintended consequences is hard. And if a company like Amazon can't pull it off without problems, it's difficult to imagine that less sophisticated companies can."

Because tech is so insular, and because most of my friends work in tech, in my head, I'm imagining one of my techie friends saying, "Well, that's Amazon; *I* could do it."

To you, I'd ask, well, how would you start? What would you do differently? How would you write code that allows for inclusivity in a program required to exclude people based on any number of specific factors? I'm not saying your program wouldn't run; I'm saying it will exclude people needed so desperately in tech and other STEM fields by filtering out data that you wouldn't normally see. The stakes are too high to get this wrong, and getting it wrong is already disproportionately penalizing already marginalized groups. We need those voices in the room when we are developing these technologies. I hear the promises that AI will be the silver bullet of staffing, and perhaps it may someday. For it to work, I'm saying it will need to get to a place where it works by prioritizing inclusivity.

So go prove me wrong. When developing a plan to put AI in place for hiring, the Center for Equity, Gender & Leadership makes the following recommendations.[90]

On Your Teams

- Enable diverse and multidisciplinary teams working on algorithms and AI systems.
- Promote a culture of ethics and responsibility related to AI.

---

90   Genevieve Smith and Ishita Rustagi, "Mitigating Bias in Artificial Intelligence the Snapshot an Equity Fluent Leadership Playbook," *Berkley Haas* (July 2020), https://haas.berkeley.edu/wp-content/uploads/UCB_Playbook_Snapshot_R10_V2_spreads2.pdf.

For Your AI Model

- Practice responsible dataset development.
- Establish policies and practices that enable responsible algorithm development.

For Leadership

- Establish corporate governance for responsible AI and end-to-end internal policies to mitigate bias.
- Engage corporate social responsibility (CSR) to advance responsible/ethical AI and larger systems change.

Use your voice and influence to advance industry change and regulations for responsible AI. I'm here for it.

Inclusive Interviews

In 2012, when I was in my twenties, I had the hardest job interview I've had to date.

I was applying to become a child advocate for the City of Atlanta for the summer. It was prestigious, coveted, and unpaid. Only law students had ever been accepted, and the City told me so when they called me to interview. Only people who could afford to live without being paid for 40-hour weeks were eligible. They were also clear that participants in this program had come from the best local schools including HBCUs. The program was educational, experience heavy, out in the field, and "never give less than 100%" for the program's clients. And those clients were children suffering from basically what I went through, or worse. Every bit of work impacted a child's life. I sat across the table from three Black women: clearly powerhouses who were smart, amazing examples of advocacy. On the inside, I was praying I'd used enough deodorant and had nothing in my teeth while wondering, *What am I doing here?*

"Well, you aren't in law school, and am I right in thinking that you haven't even completed your undergrad yet?" one interviewer asked.

"That is correct, but I am going into my senior year," I said.

"You understand that if we were to take you on, you would be held to the same standard as actual law students?" she asked. "We can't ask one of our lawyers to be without support just to have you be here over a law student."

"I am prepared to work as hard as I need to, to be the best," I said. And I was.

I was asked to get into as much detail as I felt comfortable sharing about my time in foster care. The interviewers asked me thoughtful questions about my experience with guardian al litems, advocates, and lawyers on my case. I shared more than I had intended to, and more than I ever had or likely will again in a professional setting, hoping they'd see I belonged there.

Mostly, they were curious about me.

The eldest lawyer at the table, who I assumed to be the boss because she spoke the least, finally interrupted:

"I hope you'll forgive the way I ask this," she said, "but how are you here?"

I could feel them all watching me intently. I took a deep breath and closed my eyes for a moment before responding.

"I just want to be like everyone else," I said. "I just want to be able to earn the same opportunities as people who haven't gone through the same things as me. I don't want to be given anything I didn't earn, but I do want to be treated the same. It's hard to be shut out of opportunities because of decisions you don't make for yourself. I've always been willing to work to show people I'm a good bet. So here I am."

As they thanked me for my time, I think I may have even bowed a little on the way out. When I got home, I threw the blouse I'd been sweating through in the trash. I opened my laptop to thank the interviewers as I assumed it would be the last time I heard from them, but there was a message waiting for me:

"Dear Di, thank you so much for your time earlier today and for sharing your story. I think I can speak for all of us when I say your story is inspiring. While none of us felt it would be fair to ask any attorneys to take you on over a law student, we do feel as a group that your experience makes you one of the most valuable candidates we saw. Because of that, we've decided to extend you an offer to join the summer child advocacy internship program. We won't have a desk for you, and you'll have to go through the training program at Emory's Law School at the same speed as the law students before you can come aboard, but you belong here. We hope you'll join us."

Whoa. This was a crucial turning point for me. It's hard for many people to understand how much impact interactions within something as meaningless as a job interview can be. True, they weren't paying me, and it didn't cost them anything to extend me that opportunity except for their time and expertise. But they were willing to include me. They were willing to teach me and treat me the same as everyone else, and it mattered to me.

When I talk about inclusion, this is what I mean. I'm talking about seeing that maybe what we've been taught about who "the best possible candidate" is has been skewed based on the systems that we don't see. Systems that shut people like me and others out wholesale to the detriment of companies seeking exactly our skills and experience.

When I worked for the first time with a tech group in Silicon Valley, one of the first questions I got was, "Did you go to Berkeley or Stanford?" The way people posed the question assumed one of those outcomes. Hiring managers and companies think they're doing the right thing by excluding people because they "only want the best."

But I have some news for you. According to Scott E. Page and his book *The Diversity Bonus*, smart people educated in the same way by the same schools and the same classes are smart in the same way.[91] They also fail to solve problems differently, innovate less, and get stuck on problems *in the same place*. The same people create the same viewpoint, the same perspectives, and the same outcomes. They create echo chambers. If you want to do better than everyone else, "the same" will not get you there. That's science.

How Do We Make This Process More Inclusive?

As far back as the early 2010s, Google announced it was researching how to make its interview be more inclusive of people and, ideally, remove more interviewer bias. Google's hiring team was smart in using a rubric system to compare each candidate. While still imperfect, this forced people to figure out in advance what the truly required qualifications for each open position were—the must-haves versus the nice-to-haves. Each person on the hiring team was required to score each candidate and write down what they liked or didn't like about their candidacy. While this slowed down hiring in some cases, and maybe annoyed candidates who wanted the system to move faster, it also cut out a lot of bias they had been seeing. When people were forced to consider and write down what they thought rather than just voting yes or no on a candidate, suddenly folks couldn't "just know" or rely on their "gut" (read: biases).

But as usual, this only matters if the hiring team is likewise inclusive and diverse. Three people in a room who share the same biases, identities, perspectives, and experiences will likely come to the same conclusions about the candidate and agree with and validate each other that it's not "because of biases," but because of "culture" or "fit."

---

91 Scott E Page, *The Diversity Bonus How Great Teams Pay off in the Knowledge Economy* (Princeton University Press, 2019).

Another tactic that has been pretty successful in tech is for the HR/ hiring team/system to keep track of the quality of the interviewers and not just the candidates. Basically, you put together a diverse slate of candidates, and then you record the direction each interviewer went and why. For candidates who are hired, keep track of how they're doing: Are they a good fit? Are they awesome at their jobs? If yes, the interviewer gets a high score and keeps interviewing for the company—Amazon calls these folks who both interview well and have specific hiring and inclusion training their (aptly named) "bar raisers."

I sat in on an interview process for a Black candidate at a start-up tech company—let's call it Glacier—a few years ago. Glacier had been accused of bias and wanted me to assure them this was not the case. Could I see if they had any other solvable problems that stood out to me? So I began observing the hiring process, during which the candidate was required to present to the tech team on their work to date or a project they were proud of.

As one particular candidate got up and began talking, I looked around the table. The hiring team—several white men and two Indian men—had their laptops open and were clearly not listening. The candidate wasn't excited by this and told them so. In fact, he would later email the hiring team that their behavior had been racist. The hiring team hurried to assure each other that this was not the case. They said the candidate was angry at not being hired and was "playing the race card." I disagreed. I'd seen the other interviews. I saw how they granted respect and attention to white male candidates. They reserved comments about someone not being "technical" enough or "too shrill" or "not a good culture fit" for women or people of color. Obviously, they weren't thrilled with me, and I was accused of "having an agenda."

I *did* have an agenda. I wanted them to do better and be able to look at their process more critically as outsiders might see it and make improvements. Since then, four of Glacier's 25 employees have come to me separately to discuss how they might improve company culture from the inside. Otherwise, they'll leave the company entirely. Imagine what that turnover costs versus some humility and improvements I could've made might have cost them. Instead, they decided that there were no qualified women+ or people of color for the position.

When I was working in the advertising department, I was 29 years old. My boss, who was a woman, wanted to introduce me to everyone and told our coworkers I was going to do big things. I thought this was my dream job and that I had finally made it. I was a senior photographer with one junior photographer under me. I had a big office, all the perks.

About a year in, we were hiring, and I was interviewing potential candidates. A leading candidate was a mom with a son who was three. My boss said, "Don't hire her, she's a mother and will need to leave to pick kids up—dead end." I wasn't a mom, and since she wasn't the candidate I had planned to hire anyway, I didn't give it much thought. I became pregnant myself and had a miscarriage. I was devastated. I told my boss, because I felt I had to take some time off, and suddenly everything about our relationship changed. Rather than being supportive, she was dismissive and aloof.

When I became pregnant again, not so long after, she became openly hostile. I was being left off emails and projects, and my boss was lobbying to get my direct report into my larger office. I told my boss I was uncomfortable, and she very publicly shouted an obscenities-laden tirade at me for 45 minutes about not being a team player. Other coworkers overheard it and went with me to report what had happened to HR, which only made matters worse for me because HR set up a plan where my boss and I were forced into weekly mediation where I felt totally ganged up on. I wasn't allowed to transfer off her team because, according to HR, "She was trying." She wasn't trying. She just became more and more hostile.

Finally, when the company experienced a downsizing, I was let go. My direct report stayed, my boss stayed, and everyone else on my team stayed. If I could go back and change anything, it would have been to not report to HR; they made everything worse and covered for my bully and eventually let her fire me without cause. I was let go with a severance based on not suing them, and I was a new mother, so I had to take it.

—L.J., national office supply company

Employee Benefits

When I help companies become more inclusive with benefits packages, I always look beyond the standard health care and paid vacation policies. Yes, those things are nice, but employees, especially millennial and Gen Z employees, expect a company to share their values. How do you show each individual you share their values when the things that are important to them can be so different? This is one of the places where the difference between equity and equality comes in, and for help with that, I interviewed a friend: Sarah Bedrick, a cofounder at Compt.

With Compt, companies decide on a predetermined investment, on a predetermined cycle, and then together they define categories of spending within employee benefits packages. These can be anything—continuous learning, family, charitable giving, student loan assistance, health, and wellness. A company pays a set amount, each employee logs in, and it works similar to a bank account where they can spend the money on what's important to them. It's entirely vendorless. Many benefits packages have a collection of vendors they work with, like a catalogue, which don't include local gyms, yoga studios, or other community businesses. Compt has helped change all that by making benefits packages more inclusive, equitable, and fair.

"Inclusive employee benefits improve employee experience at all levels," says Compt. "It also helps companies with their engagement, recruiting, and retention. Traditionally, employee benefits have been lopsided, as in they only solve for certain types of people. In the old days, we'd have beer and Ping Pong as employee perks, and that attracted more beer drinkers and Ping Pong players. Like attracts like. But then some people would say, 'Well, I don't drink beer,' and you'd add cider to be more inclusive, or then people would say, 'I don't drink cider,' and you'd add wine to be more inclusive. But then some people would say, 'Well, I don't drink,' and you'd find yourself starting to think about, well, what about those people? Or what about people who can't attend happy hour because they have children; or, as is more and more common, millennials taking care of a parent at home—what do those folks do? What are we telling them by not including them? That they don't belong here. How does that impact their career trajectory? How does that impact their goals for themselves?"

> *"If we were to build the workforce from scratch today, we wouldn't build what we have in place."*
> —**Sarah Bedrick**, Compt

We don't, as business owners, want to be defining for people what should be important to them based on the narrow lens of what's important to us and assume one size fits all. The big idea is letting people decide for themselves what's important and showing more ways for folks to bring their most authentic selves to work and build community with other coworkers who share their interests.

Executive Recruiters

One of the major problems for staffing in tech and other STEM fields is that the people holding all the C-Team jobs are executive recruiters. An executive recruiter is an experienced professional who leverages their own network to create pools of candidates for top positions within a company and does the headhunting, vetting, and research for candidates. Executive recruiters are often paid a fee equal to one-third of the executive's first-year salary.

For a company that doesn't have its own experienced internal staffing, this can be a good deal, but there's a catch: most of these staffing companies have their own diversity issues that mirror the issues of the companies they are staffing for, and since executive recruiters pull from their own networks, the pools of candidates tend to be decidedly monochromatic. Until the way that these searches are conducted changes, or the people working at the top of these companies change, that's likely to stay the same.

"The start-ups are just as bad as the big companies, and the big companies are terrible," noted former senior recruiter for Alphabet Amy Vernetti, who is quoted in an article featured on *Champions of Diversity.* "Executive recruiters who authentically understand this issue—I don't know if there are any."[92]

Longtime software executive Lucinda Duncalfe adds in the *Champions of Diversity* article, "We can't look to organizations that are less diverse than the tech firms to solve the tech diversity problem."

While many companies are now seeking help to expand the diversity of their candidate pools, they must also be careful they don't fall into old, comfortable, and unproductive patterns. If you use a recruiting company, make sure it represents your DEI ambitions. Recruiters must know you won't be selecting a candidate until you have a diverse pool of qualified applicants. Otherwise, nothing changes.

---

92 "Techs Hidden Diversity Problem: Executive Headhunters," Champions of Diversity, July 3, 2020, https://championsofdiversity.info/2020/07/03/techs-hidden-diversity-problem-executive-headhunters/.

"I've seen companies whose job descriptions and careers pages mention hot-tub hangouts and regular alcohol-centered activities be confused about why they struggle attracting a qualified, diverse pool of applicants."

—**Jennifer Kim**, Startup advisor, Head of People, and Diversity & Inclusion strategist

Whiteboard Interviews

I know we discussed this a little earlier with stereotype threat, but it bears repeating. We need to find a way to get rid of whiteboard interviews. North Carolina State recently released a study testing how candidates did in public whiteboard interviews and found that the only thing they test is anxiety. Furthermore, they are incredibly biased. Study author Chris Parnin, assistant computer science professor at North Carolina State writes: "For example, interviewers may give easier problems to candidates they prefer. But the format may also serve as a barrier to entire classes of candidates. For example, in our study, all of the women who took the public interview failed, while all of the women who took the private interview passed. Our study was limited, and a larger sample size would be needed to draw firm conclusions, but the idea that the very design of the interview process may effectively exclude an entire class of job candidates is troubling."[93]

They also found that between the candidates who were given "traditional" whiteboard interviews and those who were able to interview in private, candidates given whiteboard interviews did half as well. But we already knew this; so let's try harder.

---

93 North Carolina State University, "Tech Sector Job Interviews Assess Anxiety, Not Software Skills," ScienceDaily, accessed January 26, 2021, https://www.sciencedaily.com/releases/2020/07/200714101228.htm.

TL;DR:

- Improve your job descriptions. Use welcoming language, be genuine, and be better than other companies hiring for the same position.

- Enable diverse and multidisciplinary teams working on algorithms and AI systems.

- Promote a culture of ethics and responsibility related to AI.

- Practice responsible dataset development for your AI model, and establish policies and practices that enable responsible algorithm development.

- Establish corporate governance for responsible AI and end-to-end internal policies to mitigate bias.

- Engage CSR to advance responsible/ethical AI and larger systems change.

- We have a skewed perspective on "the best possible candidate," based on the systems that we don't see. Systems that shut people like me and others out wholesale to the detriment of companies seeking exactly our skills and experience.

- Let people decide for themselves what's important, and show more ways for folks to bring their most authentic selves to work and build community with other coworkers who share their interests.

Chapter 6

ONBOARDING

B y now, it should be pretty obvious that an inclusive workplace is critical for a company's overall success. Inclusion drives everything. When employees are more involved in their team, it drives retention, which creates more recruitment opportunities. Happy and supported employees bring their network to your door, which increases brand love, which increases the number of awesome employees accepting offers to work with your team.

"Onboarding is a pivotal moment for making employees feel included from day one," writes Sonja Gittens-Ottley in *Wavelength*. "It sets the tone for a person's tenure at your company, laying the foundation for their knowledge of and experience working for your company. This is why building an inclusive onboarding experience is so important to creating an inclusive company culture."[94]

---

94 Sonja Gittens-Ottley, "Inclusion Starts on Day One: 10 Ways to Build an Inclusive Onboarding Experience," Wavelength by Asana, March 14, 2018, https://wavelength.asana.com/inclusive-onboarding-experience/.

Onboarding and Orientation Are Not the Same Thing

Often, employers—36% of them, according to one study[95]—rely solely on HR orientation as the entire process for transitioning a new hire to a full-capacity employee. Let's look at it this way, instead: If an interstate highway is all of your employees running at full speed, then onboarding is your on-ramp. Onboarding gives your new employee time to get up to speed and feel like they are part of the fabric of your company, rather than an "other." It is a critical stage in an employee's lifecycle with your company.

Most people know some of the infamously misogynist practices of this company. But this was before that. When I joined, I was a female engineer, one of the few, and I thought I was somewhere cool. I used the company['s product] myself. During my onboarding process, there was a huge group, and we did ice-breaking and team-building activities together. I thought that was pretty awesome. I'd never done that with a company as part of onboarding. Usually, it's just getting your machine and finding out where the bathrooms are.

Something that made me feel weird off the bat, though, was the woman from HR letting us all know that we weren't allowed to date the somewhat famous tech leaders in the Valley. Then she made a little pout with her face. I heard a lot of the guys in the group chuckle. I thought to myself, You have to be kidding me. Gross. No one is here for that. But when I looked around for reassurance, I saw basically no one who looked like me, so I pasted a smile on my face and let it go. I should've known.

---

95   Kronos, "Making the Most of Your Onboarding Processes," *Kronos*, accessed January 26, 2021, https://www.kronos.com/resources/new-hire-momentum-driving-onboarding-experience-research-report.

Things got worse. During my first week, my direct manager's messages started getting flirty. I brushed them off, mentioned I had a boyfriend, and he replied that he had a girlfriend as well and they were in an "open relationship." I pretended to be increasingly busy, but he didn't let up. Anytime we were alone, he made sexual comments. I let it go. I didn't want to be that woman. I had seen what happened to her here in the Valley. She tells her story, and people think she's lying for money or attention or worse. I would have no allies. My career would be over. I would have a black mark on my career for life.

Gross messages turned into inappropriate comments, which turned into touching me whenever he could. Shoulder rubs that I didn't want. Brushing himself up against me when he passed by me in a meeting or literally anywhere in the office. I tried everything I could think of to make it stop. I tried to never be alone. I told other women what was happening only to find out that he (or others) had done the same thing to them. We made pacts to stay together, to eat together, to leave together. It didn't matter. He found a way.

Finally, I tried to get off his team; I'd gotten a good review, and I put in for a transfer. Then he went back in and changed my review to keep me on his team. There was no way out of this. I had to go to HR—mistake. They told me I'd probably "unknowingly" instigated it. They told me that this was the culture in the Valley, and I wasn't going to survive if I couldn't "take a joke." They told me they would talk to him, but since this was his first offense and he was a "high performer," likely nothing would be done. I was floored. This wasn't his first offense! I told the HR rep so. I told her that I knew for a fact that other women had reported him.

"Which other women?" they asked, because HR reports are private and confidential, and the company might be sued for breaching his privacy.

I told them that I didn't feel comfortable saying, and suddenly I was the liar. I was the one who had no proof. I was the troublemaker.

I was devastated. All I wanted was to do the work I loved, be in the career I had worked my ass off to get to, and there I was being told I was a hysterical liar. They did nothing. He was enraged that I had reported him and took to berating me in public and in private whenever he could...Finally, I had to quit. I moved on to a women-founded company and I'm happy here. But to my knowledge, he and his buddies are still there, still sexually harassing women and getting no consequences from HR. That was the job that let me know that HR isn't there to protect the employees; it's there to protect the company.

—T.J., large transportation company

Need more proof of the connection between onboarding and greater employee engagement and retention? Companies without a well-planned onboarding process lose 17% of their new hires within the first three months.[96] And 69% of employees are more likely to stay with a company if they've had a positive onboarding experience.[97] Yeah, onboarding matters. A lot.

---

96 Roy Maurer, "Onboarding Key to Retaining, Engaging Talent," SHRM (April 16, 2015), https://www.shrm.org/resourcesandtools/hr-topics/talent-acquisition/pages/onboarding-key-retaining-engaging-talent.aspx.

97 Arlene S Hirsch, "Don't Underestimate the Importance of Good Onboarding," SHRM (August 10, 2017), https://www.shrm.org/resourcesandtools/hr-topics/talent-acquisition/pages/dont-underestimate-the-importance-of-effective-onboarding.aspx. https://www.kronos.com/resources/new-hire-momentum-driving-onboarding-experience-research-report

As T.J.'s story above shows, the "on-ramp" of onboarding can quickly veer in the wrong direction when companies include sexual innuendo or other blatant discrimination.

Then there's the recent consult I had with a CTO, which went like this.

CTO: I have to ask you about a nightmare situation here. A friend of mine was telling me a story about how a nonbinary person at another tech company is suing the company for discrimination. Basically, they came on as an SE1 and decided not to improve in any way. There was a programming language they didn't know and wouldn't learn, just super toxic, and so the company brought in someone to help—a white guy—and they made him an SE2, and that just made the situation worse. The company ultimately decided to fire them. And now, they are suing for discrimination. That's a nightmare, that people can just sue for discrimination when they were the one at fault, right? Just because they're nonbinary?

Me: Well, actually, I disagree. How did this situation get to where it got? So you say this person came in as an SE1, what specifically would have been done if this person was a white guy?

CTO: Well, the company would get him the help he needed to learn the language. His manager would be checking in with him. He would be helped through any trouble he was having, and probably he'd have a mentor. Both of those people would be keeping the CTO up to date on issues and or progress.

Me: And why didn't that happen with this person?

CTO: I dunno, probably they didn't want to do anything wrong and took a more hands-off approach.

Me: And why was that?

CTO: Because they were different from what the company had experienced before.

Me: And how did that work out for the employee?

CTO: They didn't get the help they needed, they didn't get the mentorship they needed, and the team kept the CTO totally in the dark.

Me: And then hired a white guy over them to do the work the company needed.

CTO: Right.

Me: So is that discrimination?

CTO: Yes. It definitely is.

Me: Is that how you would've handled the situation?

CTO: No. Not at all. You're right. If it was just some guy, it would've been totally different. That was fully discrimination.

Me: And?

CTO: They should be sued.

Me: So not a nightmare situation then, huh?

CTO: It was for the employee.

Me: Absolutely.

CTO: I'm glad we pay you.

Me: That's right. Tell your friends.

A new software engineer joined the lab, except that unknown to me, he wasn't really a software engineer. He was a data analyst who wanted to move into software engineering and was hired on the basis that he would learn on the job. I sat down and made him a really nice learning plan that would cost him less than $100 to complete for his job.

He flat out refused to do it, stating he didn't have enough time. He was a single dude with no kids, no family obligations, no illnesses, nothing that would prevent him from spending a few hours a week on courses. To really hammer this home, he constantly complained that he wasn't working on anything and didn't have anything to do and why wasn't I just handing him stuff. So he could have done the courses during working hours.

It was so weird because I actually like him and think he's a nice guy, oblivious, not actively harmful. Instead of management telling this guy, "Hey, buckle up and get these courses done, this is what you were hired to do," I was told to "coach him" and "hold his hand." I was seriously told to hold a grown man's hand to get him through a codebase.

I said, "No, not unless you're planning to make me a manager or senior staff, because they were essentially expecting me to be this guy's technical manager without pay, and to do that on top of my regular job...We have to work so much harder to prove ourselves, and then when the time comes for advancement, we get passed up or told to mentor the men that have been picked out as golden children to get them ahead.

—T.D., research lab

Onboarding the Right Way

The right way of onboarding, I've found, includes these strategies from battle-tested employee engagement programs.

Tap into online tools. If you're a smaller company, sites such as Enboarder and Culture Amp offer platforms for creating inclusive onboarding experiences. You can collect, understand, and use data throughout an employee's lifecycle. Enboarder.com has solutions for remote onboarding, and even "reboarding" for transitions back to work after events such as COVID-19.

Batch hire. If you're a bigger company, batch hiring is best. It creates cohorts who can go through onboarding together and doesn't create the "othering" or "new person" tense space between members of your team.

Use the buddy system. Companies doing onboarding right all have some sort of buddy system or mentor program. Each new hire gets a "buddy" to be their partner as they get up to speed. Eventually, new hires who've earned some seniority will volunteer to be buddies themselves.

As an example, New York University[98] outlines the characteristics of a buddy:

Communicator: A buddy should encourage open communication. The buddy should provide relevant information to the new employee and encourage a process of continued, self-directed learning.

Role Model: The buddy should be a model employee and exemplify NYU values.

Motivated: The buddy should have a positive outlook on his/her work and use that perspective to help build self-confidence and loyalty in the new employee. The buddy should lead by example.

Strong Performer: The buddy can help guide the new employee in many situations based on his/her experience and knowledge obtained in the work environment.

> *"An inclusive onboarding experience is like adding someone to your game of musical chairs: You can't add someone new without stopping the music and adding a chair. Creating a meaningful experience means slowing down, making adjustments, and including your new hire."*
>
> **—Sonja Gittens-Ottley**

Help them move from outsider to insider. Create programs that help new hires go from the outside to an insider. This includes not only the new hire's projects and where the bathrooms are but also the team

---

98 New York University, "New Employee Onboarding: Buddy Guidelines," *NYU,* 2006, https://www.nyu.edu/content/dam/nyu/hr/documents/managerguides/BuddyGuidelines.pdf.

lexicon, including acronyms, abbreviations, etc. In order to be inclusive (and effective), you should be able to take someone from fresh off the street to secret handshake in short order.

Introduce to ERGs. We've already discussed ERGs and their importance within a company. But it would go a long way toward inclusivity if, for example, the leader of a parenting ERG personally invited a new hire to lunch. Small action, big impact. It also has the secondary benefit of showing a new hire how important building an inclusive culture is to your company.

Prep your team. Prepping your team on goals and expectations for the new-hire onboard is crucial. Everyone is different and will need different tools to be successful within your organization. So make sure you are choosing the right onboarding team to make that employee feel welcome and included from day one. Every hour that you spend on onboarding pays off in retention and culture.

Create a feedback system. While you should hear plenty of positive comments about your onboarding, this also helps address problems that inevitably arise. Let's say a new hire has a run-in with a manager whose creepy behavior you've been unaware of. Employees need to know how to report and where to get support from day one. Otherwise, they may just leave without ever reporting the issue, opening you up to never-ending problems from recruitment to lawsuits.

Provide a "new city" guide. Support the new hires who are coming from, or relocating to, a different city. As Sarah Cordivano writes on Medium,[99] cutting through the red tape can alleviate the mental burden. She suggests sharing information about:

---

99 Sarah Cordivano, "Understanding and Designing an Inclusive Onboarding Experience.," Medium, December 17, 2019, https://medium.com/@sarah. cordivano/understanding-and-designing-an-inclusive-onboarding-experience-4be6b5f7c669.

- Religious spaces for prayer
- Instructions on how to enroll children in kindergarten or school
- Location of cultural institutions
- How to get in touch with police or other emergency services
- How to find general practitioners or specialty doctors (especially in an emergency)
- Health community spaces including those that offer special healthcare such as HIV+ support, PrEP, STD testing, and other counseling
- Queer and LGBTQI+ community spaces
- Spaces that offer mental health support (finding a therapist is a particular challenge in some areas and can take months to sort out.)

Make Onboarding Ongoing
During the Employee's First Year

Onboarding should be a lot more than a quick round of introductions, an ID badge, and a tour of the office on an employee's first day. It should start during the prehire process and continue throughout an employee's first year. It should provide training and support, and opportunities for the employee to offer feedback.

Think of prehire conversations as the start of the onboarding process. Be clear with applicants and interviewees about what your company expects of them, and what they can expect of your company. Discuss leadership approaches, how decisions are made, collaborative working methods, communication, and how your company handles dispute resolution.

During initial training, use a clearly structured and well-documented process to make sure you cover your company's code of conduct and antiharassment policy as well as policies and procedures for working across the company and in their specific departments. Emphasize the company's shared values while also recognizing the contributions people from diverse backgrounds bring to the table—this isn't about assimilation with rigid norms but a collaborative approach to working together. Over the course of the year, use check-ins and refresher training to help people internalize your company's values. Make trainings thoughtful and interactive with real-life examples, instead of interactive videos that are generic and dreaded. — Project Include[100]

TL;DR:

- Onboarding and orientation are not the same thing.
- The HR Department does the onboarding for 36% of companies.
- A pleasant onboarding experience makes 69% of employees more likely to stay with a company.
- You should have policies and practices surrounding your onboarding that can take a new employee from off the street to insider. They shouldn't vary wildly based on managers.
- Keep onboarding up throughout the first year.
- Onboard people in the context of their whole lives. If they need help finding schools for their kids, places to worship, or places that cater to dietary restrictions, you can promote inclusion by supporting them as whole people outside of their work duties.

---

100 "Employee Lifecycle," Project Include, accessed January 27, 2021, https://projectinclude.org/employee_lifecycle#make-onboarding-ongoing-during-the-employees-first-year. "Make onboarding ongoing during the employee's first year" subheading.

Chapter 7

BUILDING TEAMS AND
TRACKING PERFORMANCE

W hen I was at Georgia State University, I realized I was a natural leader with a gravitational pull toward other people. I was on boards. I led clubs. To this day, people regularly accost me about joining and leading committees. I can figure out where people's gaps are and fill them in. I can lead; I make a good second; or I can follow as needed. At Georgia State, I knew when I built teams, they would become better than the sum of their parts.

As it turns out, I'm not magical—I've been employing organizational psychology when I build teams. Including my own.

Building Teams

Teams over Stars

How important are teams versus individuals? An amazing 2006 study[101] was published in *Management Science* tracking individual cardiac

---

101 Robert S. Huckman and Gary P. Pisano, "The Firm Specificity of Individual Performance: Evidence from Cardiac Surgery," *Management Science* 52, no. 4

surgeons' patient mortality rate at 43 different hospitals. It was thought at the start of the study that surgeons could freelance and their skills and talents would be largely portable and travel with them, but after analyzing nearly 40,000 surgeries, it turns out surgeons weren't getting better with practice *individually*. What they found was that surgery was a team process and that with practice the *team* got better. But when a surgeon moved on or joined a new hospital, they went right back to the start again, even with all the surgeries under their belt. Again, with practice on the same team, they would again get better.

Similarly, a 2008 study by Groysberg, Lee, and Nanda[102] examined the transferability of "star quality" of high-performing securities analysts. They found the exact same thing. Stars were only stars on their home team. Once they left and joined a new team, on average, it took them five years to regain their "star" status.

Why does this matter when we talk about building teams? Well, as we discussed in the hiring chapter of this book, common practice has always been to set standards, to exclude, to get as many star individual contributors at your business and they will make the best teams. But do they? Research suggests not really.

Huckman and Staats reaffirmed their "teams over stars" hypothesis in 2009[103] by taking it to tech. On a team of software developers, team familiarity (how frequently a team had worked together in the past) was a better predictor of team success than how many stars were on the team.

(April 2006): 473–88, https://doi.org/10.1287/mnsc.1050.0464.

102 Boris Groysberg, Linda-Eling Lee, and Ashish Nanda, "Can They Take It with Them? The Portability of Star Knowledge Workers' Performance," *Management Science* 54, no. 7 (July 2008): 1213–30, https://doi.org/10.1287/mnsc.1070.0809.

103 Robert S. Huckman and Bradley R. Staats, "Fluid Tasks and Fluid Teams: The Impact of Diversity in Experience and Team Familiarity on Team Performance," *Harvard Business School Working Paper* 09-145 (2009), https://www.hbs.edu/faculty/Publication%20Files/09-145_02c7d6af-93df-473a-aac2-fdd7bff28055.pdf.

"Today, too many teams are temporary: people collaborate on a single project and never work together again," writes Adam Grant in *Originals: How Non-Conformists Move the World*.[104] "Teams need the opportunity to learn about each other's capabilities and develop productive routines. So once we get the right people on the bus, let's make sure they spend some time driving together."

Building Charismatic Teams

Let's look at a study for *Harvard Business Review*[105] measuring successful teams. When searching for the "it" factor that predicted successful teams, researchers had employees in a call center wear badges that acted as tools to measure contact. What they ultimately found was that the best predictor was communication. Or, more accurately, charisma on a team. The following factors were found to be the measurable ones to use as a guide or rubric:

1. Everyone on the team talks and listens in roughly equal measure, keeping contributions short and sweet.

2. Members face one another, and their conversations and gestures are energetic.

3. Members connect directly with one another—not just with the team leader.

4. Members carry on back-channel or side conversations within the team.

5. Members periodically break, go exploring outside the team, and bring information back.

---

104 Adam Grant, *Originals How Non-Conformists Move the World*, with a foreword by Sheryl Sandberg (New York: Penguin Books, 2017).
105 Alex Pentland, "The New Science of Building Great Teams," *Harvard Business Review*, April 1, 2012, https://hbr.org/2012/04/the-new-science-of-building-great-teams?referral=03759&cm_vc=rr_item_page.bottom.

Individual talent, as mentioned above, is less of a factor than previously thought when making up successful teams.

The Marshmallow Test

In a popular TED Talk,[106] Tom Wujec describes what is known commonly as "the marshmallow test." When Wujec discovered this test, created by Peter Skillman several years ago, he loved it and turned it into a design workshop for businesses and leaders.

The premise is that teams of four have to build the tallest "free-standing" structure in 18 minutes, with the following items:

- 1 marshmallow
- 20 sticks of uncooked spaghetti
- 1 yard of tape
- 1 yard of string

At the end of the 18 minutes, the marshmallow must be on top. As Wujec explains, most teams orient themselves to the task (and jockey for power). Then they plan and build. At the very end, one person gingerly places the marshmallow on top of the structure, stands back and says "ta-da!" and everyone watches as the structure falls over.

Who consistently does the worst at this? Business school graduates. Who consistently does the best? Kindergarteners.

Seriously. Why? Because they spend less of the time planning (or jockeying for power) and spend more of the time tinkering. That way, they know earlier which points of the structure are working throughout the project. Business school graduates are trained to find the single right answer and then execute it. Then they commonly run

---

106 Tom Wujec, "Build a Tower, Build a Team," TED, February 2010, TED video, 6:37, https://www.ted.com/talks/tom_wujec_build_a_tower_build_a_team#t-96857

out of time, and it's a crisis. Sounds familiar, right? Another interesting fact about this project is that architects and engineers commonly do the best (because: science!). The CEOs are average—but if the CEO has an admin on their team, then they do significantly better because the admin is acting as a facilitator. So the best teams are those with specialized skills but also a facilitator—someone who is managing the project.[107]

After leading this challenge for several teams around the country, Tom Wujec decided to up the ante. He added stakes. There would now be a prize. The prize would be $10,000 worth of software to the team with the tallest structure. Guess what happened? Every team failed. Not a single structure was standing at the end of the 18 minutes. As it turns out, high stakes negatively impact creativity.

Why does the marshmallow challenge matter? Because when we talk about teams, sometimes they're pick-up teams that don't usually work together, have a shared lexicon, or shared experiences and that can act against us and provide deeper challenges. It's important to manage for that, especially when it comes to judging performance equally.

DiSC Test

Based on the work of American psychologist William Moulton Marston,[108] the DiSC test measures personality types for people (and thus teams). As the model below demonstrates, it focuses on four primary emotions and associated behavioral responses. We identify them today as D (dominance), I (influence), S (steadiness), and C (conscientiousness). These tests are pretty popular in tech team circles, so I'll break the parts down.

---

107 Cue collective snort from our project managers!
108 Fun fact about Marston: he went by the pen name Charles Moulton and created the character of Wonder Woman having been inspired by suffragettes (and centerfolds, apparently). Isn't life fun?

D is considered a dominant personality—"Type A." They are usually pretty demanding and can sometimes seem immovable. They like to take charge, they make decisions quickly, and they like immediate results, which can make them impatient. They have trouble with folks who are a little more "go with the flow" than themselves, which can sometimes put them at odds with folks who fall into the yellow area of personality. They also have difficulty remembering to listen to other peoples' ideas and remembering to give others an opportunity to speak in a group setting. Still, people are often attracted to D types, who can make good leaders if they don't lean too far into their lesser qualities.

I personalities are sunny, social, and go with the flow. They have trouble taking things seriously and will often seek social situations as a way to de-stress. They love to talk, they make friends easily, and they have many friends. These are your extroverts. They love to help and create inclusive environments. Seek out your I personality types when thinking about how to make the workplace more comfortable for everyone. They also don't like to be criticized, especially in public, so if you have to do so, remember to speak with them in private and use a compliment sandwich as a supporting tool. Also, watch out for these types becoming overcommitted and unable to deliver. They like to say yes.

S personalities are the facilitators. The supporters. They don't get frazzled in difficult situations, and they often find themselves acting as a mediator. This person is often a good group center and will work hard to maintain harmony within group settings. They can also have trouble saying no, so leaders with a green on their team will need to watch out for that tendency and help them prioritize. Because they want to maintain harmony in a group, it can also work against them if it keeps them from making hard decisions.

C personalities are perfectionists. They like order, discipline, and rationality. They are diplomatic and analytical. They like situations where they are creating precise order for standards, protocols, and other precise activities. These personalities need time to get things right, plus regular reassurance from their leaders. Praise five times as often as you critique because these folks are really sensitive to criticism.

Of course, each person is a blend of different personality types. In fact, there are about 41 identified blends of personality. (I'm about 70% S and 30% D.) Since this is a very popular team-building personality test, it's good to know where you stand and where your team stands for insights on management and conflict. If you're interested in this type of management tool, check out the *Everything DiSC Manual*.[109] There are also any number of tests available online.

Personality Test Caveat

Psychology as a field is very white, very male, and very western-medicine centered. People are hardly ever as easy or predictable as a test would have you believe, especially when we're talking about diverse teams as we are here. Now, I am not trying to ruin anyone's positive opinions about the DiSC test, as it does stand up to scientific scrutiny, but I do want people, managers especially, to be aware that trying to put team members in neat little boxes rarely goes the way you want. Use these tests as tools, but be flexible and allow for individual differences and diverse interpretations of the result.

Be Thoughtful about Inclusion When Building Teams

One voice can be silenced, but two voices together make a difference. When you don't have many members of underrepresented groups, do not intentionally separate them and put them on different teams. If you have the option, put at

---

109 Mark Scullard, PhD and Dabney Baum, EdD, *Everything DiSC® Manual*, *Discprofile.com* (Wiley, 2015), https://www.discprofile.com/products/everything-disc-manual/.

least two in a group so they have mirrors and allies, and as your company grows, use ERGs to build a supportive environment.

In the 1980s, the concept of windows and mirrors arose in designing curriculum: Educators wanted children to see themselves in the stories they heard and to learn about each other as well. Research has shown that having female peers on small teams improves the motivation, participation, and career goals of women in engineering school. This effect increases for teams that have as many women as men, and participation increases most in groups of mostly women.

Some argue that assigning people of color or women or women of color to different teams benefits the company by providing more perspective to a greater number of diverse teams. But it is at the expense of the employees from underrepresented groups. The sole member of a certain group is often expected to take on the extra and often underappreciated work of being the voice for the entire underrepresented group.

Another way to add perspectives is bringing people in from outside your company as examples of successes or connecting people across companies. If you have a speaker series or guest panels, the speakers should reflect diversity.

Participate in and sponsor tech sector organizations for underrepresented groups. It can inspire your own employees by showing that you value underrepresented groups inside the company and also provide role models for success and connections outside the company. And, it could be a lead to potential job candidates at different levels and in different functions. —Project Include[110]

---

110 "Employee Lifecycle," Project Include, accessed January 27, 2021, https://projectinclude.org/employee_lifecycle#be-thoughtful-about-inclusion-

Productive Conflict

Conflict gets a bad rap, but the worst thing a manager can do is be afraid of conflict. There are various root causes of conflict such as limited resources, unmet needs, or different values. There are definitely destructive kinds of conflict; for example, when you have team members who aren't speaking to each other and you find your facilitators managing around them. But conflict can be really productive as well. If conflict is managed as a more controlled flame rather than something burning out of control, it can create space for psychological safety and trust on a team. We do that through mediation techniques:

1. Use "I" statements: "I feel like ..."
2. Repeat what you heard: "I'm hearing you say X; is that correct?"
3. Take a breath (also known as reflective listening): No one is saying you as a person are bad. And if they are attacking you personally and not your ideas, that's quite a different matter. Sorry, #radicalcandor,[111] that's not what that means.
4. Turn down the inner monologue[112] if you have one. You are probably ascribing context to someone's opposition to you that just doesn't exist. For example, because I have an inner monologue, I can basically create a telenovela. If someone just says, "Hang on, I'm going to run your idea by the rest of the team," I hear, "You are not believable on your own." It is because you are a woman, petite, a vegan—whatever I've been "othered"

---

when-building-teams. "Be thoughtful about inclusion when building teams" subheading.
111 I've seen a lot of people sharing totally rude and unhelpful comments and ascribing them to #radicalcandor. Having read Kim Scott's book on the subject, I can tell you honestly that is not what she meant.
112 Jessica Stewart, "People Have Discovered That Not Everyone Has an Inner Monologue," My Modern Met, February 4, 2020, https://mymodernmet.com/inner-monologue/. I have an inner monologue. I just learned last year some of you don't, and it blew.me.away.

about by that person before. And maybe some of that is real, but a lot of it isn't. I'm working on it too. Try to stop.

5. **Deal with your crap.** If you lead people on any level, get yourself into therapy. I'm super serious. If you are leading people and haven't dealt with your past, you will bleed on people who didn't cut you. It happens all the time.

6. Any time you have a meeting, especially where you feel like you have to give any level of correction or criticism, ask that person what they heard you say: "Hey, Ted, can you just tell me what you heard me say? I know it's weird, but I've been finding my communication skills aren't perfect, so I want to make sure I said what I meant to."

7. Understand power dynamics. It's never okay to tell a dirty joke to someone who doesn't have the power to push back on you. No, you can't date your employees. Ever. *Because their career is at risk if they turn you down.* It's really that simple. That's not an equal power dynamic.

8. Try to imagine yourself in the other person's shoes in the context of *their* actual lives, not in the context of *your* life. Not *you* the CEO hearing something or dealing with something. I hear so many CEOs complaining about someone dealing with someone they don't or didn't have to deal with. Comparing yourself—maybe a dad with a wife and a full-time nanny—to a single mom and saying, "I have kids, and I didn't have this problem" is just tone-deaf. More people on your team relate to her over you, believe me.

9. Don't ask your lone Black employee questions you don't understand about Blackness. And while I have you: don't ask your lone Black person whether or not they feel like your culture is inclusive. I mean, what do you think they're going to say? No? "Actually, Bill, you can just take a look around?" No.

They're going to tell you it's great. They think it's obvious by their being the lone Black person. That's not okay unless it's a 10-person team. Maybe not even then.

10. If you are having conflict with someone based on their identity (and by that, I mean if *they* think it is about their identity, you likely will not agree, but you should examine that discomfort because they're probably right—even if you won't admit it), do not go to another member of that identity and try to get them on your side against that person. That's you trying to save face, not change, and take advantage of someone else's potentially disadvantaged situation. And you've taken a problem with one person and turned it into two. Change is hard; stop trying to take the easy route.

Nondisclosure and Separation Agreements

I've spoken with hundreds of people about this topic. Some people, speaking to me on the condition of anonymity, have reported truly harrowing experiences. I've promised not to reveal their names, or even the real names of the companies responsible, because people have left under separation agreements and nondisclosure agreements forbidding them from sharing their stories in a public forum. When I've asked under what conditions these legal tools would make sense, the explanations have seemed pretty unrealistic.

Nondisclosure agreements have filtered into employment agreements, especially in tech, with one-third of U.S. workers currently bound by them. According to *Harvard Business Review*, "They demand silence, often broadly worded to protect against speaking up against corporate culture or saying anything that would portray the company and its executives in a negative light."[113]

---

113 Orly Lobel, "NDAs Are out of Control. Here's What Needs to Change," *Harvard Business Review*, January 30, 2018, https://hbr.org/2018/01/ndas-are-out-of-

I'm not arguing that NDAs are totally useless, but they're largely imperfect solutions at best, and at worst they're a tool predators use to silence their own victims. If you're going to create NDAs or separation agreements, you need to make sure that person is empowered to talk about their experiences but not reveal trade secrets. The documents shouldn't be expanding; they should be getting narrower. If the only people who are in a position to turn down your severance payment with legal consequences are people who are well-off and don't need the money, you've furthered systems of oppression. According to employment discrimination lawyer Vincent White in an interview with *Fast Company*:[114] "Politicians are taking a lot of half measures. Meanwhile, what I see from finance and tech is an arms race to create the most protective NDA. These companies know they won't fix their culture issues overnight, which only emboldens them to keep deploying NDAs."

Tracking Performance

Everyone hates performance reviews. They're time-consuming, they're a minefield for managers that prefer to avoid conflict, and they're almost always full of bias. Many companies are just doing away with them completely. I understand the instinct, but pretending biases don't exist doesn't eliminate them; it makes them worse because we can't measure the issue. Take, for example, an educational video by Google Ventures. Dr. Brian Welle, Director of People Analytics, reminds us, "You can't improve what you can't measure." He describes a study in which a man and woman are working together collectively on a task. If you were a subject in their experiment, your job was to assign a value to

---

control-heres-what-needs-to-change.

114 Pavithra Mohan, "'How Much Is My Silence Worth?': Amid a Racial Reckoning, Women Are Rejecting NDAs," *Fast Company*, August 11, 2020, https://www. fastcompany.com/90529393/how-much-is-my-silence-worth-amid-a-racial-reckoning-women-are-rejecting-ndas.

the work that the employees created. There were two conditions: either you were told what each person did individually on a team, or you were told of the accomplishments of the team as a whole, and then you were expected to assign a value to each person's contributions.

Guess what happened? Well, if you were given the individual accomplishments of the man and the woman, you were more likely to assign them an equal score on a nine-point influence scale. However, if you were only given the group's accomplishments and expected to judge individual contributions on your own, you were "less likely to believe the woman had as much influence over the task as the man did."[115] What does this mean for positive outcomes such as stretch assignments and promotions? It means the more ambiguity there is in judging someone's performance, the more room there is for biases to creep in.

Types of Influencing Biases

Recency Bias is influenced by recent performance versus the performance of the entire term period. It's whatever is freshest in the manager's mind. This can be combated by tracking performance throughout someone's employment by getting peer reviews on projects, not just your own most recent experience, which can be impacted now by coronavirus, BLM protests, and a whole host of other outside influences unrelated to the workplace.

Halo Error: We often let one trait that stands out to us about an individual judge that person's entire performance. This is where identity biases creep in. If you assume a Black woman is more susceptible to anger due to stereotypes, then you can do a lot of damage to her career by letting the one time she called someone on their bad behavior (regardless of merit) impact her review if it's your job to judge her ability

---

115 Dr. Brian Welles, "Unconscious Bias @ Work | Google Ventures," *GV*, September 25, 2014, YouTube video, 1:02:50, https://www.youtube.com/watch?v=nLjFTHTgEVU.

to contribute to the team in a collaborative way. You can fight this firstly by checking your biases in this specific instance, and secondly by making sure you are measuring the multiple factors that contribute to her overall performance.

Idiosyncratic Rater Bias: Watch this: when a manager's not good at something and evaluates someone on this task, they rate the employee much higher than when evaluating them on something they themselves are great at.

When researchers Steven E. Scullen and Michael K. Mount[116] measured all of these biases, they found more than half of the variance in ratings had more to do with the personal quirks of the person rating the employee than with the employee themselves.

Share Feedback Regularly with Help from Inclusive Performance Reviews

Currently, performance reviews can be problematic by reinforcing bias, checking for "culture fit" rather than performance, and potentially limiting advancement. A process called a 360 review, wherein peers and teammates are involved in the evaluation can be political and biased. CEB found that 95% of managers are dissatisfied with the way their companies conduct performance reviews, and nearly 90% of HR leaders say the process doesn't even yield accurate information. Poorly managed performance reviews often drive good employees to leave, so be thoughtful in how you design and implement them.

Sharing feedback should be part of a process that helps employees thrive. Managers should tell employees what they're doing well, what they can improve upon, and, importantly, how

---

116 Steven E. Scullen, Michael K. Mount, and Maynard Goff, "Understanding the Latent Structure of Job Performance Ratings," *Journal of Applied Psychology* 85, no. 6 (2000): 956–70, https://doi.org/10.1037/0021-9010.85.6.956.

they can get there. Start by giving feedback regularly and clearly, with actionable items for employees. For example, if someone isn't speaking up at meetings, find out why, and set a goal to help that employee find a voice. Use regular 1:1s (usually weekly), casual check-ins, and monthly meetings to keep up a steady flow of communication.

When you have quarterly, midyear, and end-of-year performance reviews, they should provide an opportunity to review and formalize information from more casual meetings, and to look at bigger-picture career opportunities and goals. These reviews shouldn't be a tool for collecting information to fire people but a way to reinforce company values, make sure employees are set up for long-term success, and address issues as they arise.

A written overview of what was discussed helps employees set measurable goals, and nothing in the overview should be new to the employee. Information about raises and bonuses also shouldn't come as a surprise—both because your company should have a clear and transparent compensation scale and because ongoing feedback should give your employees a clear sense of how they are doing year-round. —Project Include[117]

Measuring Progress

Measuring progress is one of the six steps for building inclusive teams, writer Kathy Gurchiek shares in SHRM.[118]

---

117 "Employee Lifecycle," Project Include, accessed January 27, 2021, hhttps://projectinclude.org/employee_lifecycle#share-feedback-regularly-with-help-from-inclusive-performance-reviews. "Share feedback regularly with help from inclusive performance reviews" subheading.

118 Kathy Gurchiek, "6 Steps for Building an Inclusive Workplace," SHRM (March 19, 2018), https://www.shrm.org/hr-today/news/hr-magazine/0418/pages/6-steps-for-building-an-inclusive-workplace.aspx.

"Establish and clearly communicate specific, measurable and time-bound goals as you would with any other strategic aim," writes Gurchiek, referring to work by diversity researcher Erin Thomas, who recommends the following actions:

1. Conduct a full audit of your people processes—from recruiting and hiring to developing and retaining employees. Couple the data with engagement and other workforce survey data to gain a full measure of your climate.
2. Identify any shortcomings and measurable discrepancies around inclusiveness in your organization.
3. Instill rigor into inclusion strategies with data-driven plans, and measure the results.
4. Establish a clear business case for how the company will benefit by having a more inclusive culture by asking: *What are our inclusion goals? What are the reasons for those goals? How do we quantify inclusion? How will inclusion impact our mission, brand, or bottom line?*

As Gurchiek writes, Thomas says that "when you can answer these questions, you're speaking the language of your stakeholders, legitimizing the business of inclusion and making inclusion a 'verb' versus an ideal."

Designing Promotional Paths for a Diverse Team

A lot of folks out there are using data to fit their own sensationalized and biased narratives. In 2015, Mona Chalabi of FiveThirtyEight went on NPR to talk about "What Happens When Wives Earn More Than Husbands."[119] Chalabi tells host Rachel Martin that "in 2013, the University of Chicago Booth School of Business published a paper

---

119 Dorothy Roberts, What Happens When Wives Earn More Than Husbands, interview by Rachel Martin, NPR, February 8, 2015, https://www.npr.

that looked at 4,000 married couples in America. It found that once a woman started to earn more than her husband, divorce rates increased. Surprisingly, though, this data showed that whether the wife earns a little bit more or a lot more doesn't actually make much of a difference. So the researchers concluded from that, that what really matters is the mere fact of a woman earning more."

Here's what happened: almost every media outlet reported on these findings as "Millennial women are 'worried' about or 'ashamed' about out-earning their boyfriends or husbands!"[120] citing that NPR interview. It was everywhere, and yet no one said anything of the sort. If they did, I can't track it back through the citations.

The rest of the interview is stereotype-based innuendo. Like "Well, there must be a correlation here!" So if I may just speak on behalf of actual millennial women: no, we're not embarrassed. Pay us what we're worth, please. A mom I interviewed recently was on track to be promoted when she went on maternity leave. While she was gone, they promoted her junior, male coworker. When she returned and asked her boss why the male coworker had been promoted over her, her boss told her, "Well, we assumed when you had the baby, you wouldn't be interested in the promotion," she told me. "I was flabbergasted, Di. I mean, who doesn't want to be promoted?"

The Self-Promotion Conundrum

Google has diversity problems—it will be the first to admit it in the same way most tech companies will tell you that there is a diversity problem in tech. It's real. In an effort to promote more women, Google

org/2015/02/08/384695833/what-happens-when-wives-earn-more-than-husbands?t=1611333262340.

120 Ester Bloom, "Millennial Women Are 'Worried,' 'Ashamed' of Out-Earning Boyfriends and Husbands," *CNBC*, April 19, 2017, https://www.cnbc.com/2017/04/18/millennial-women-worry-about-out-earning-boyfriends-and-husbands.html.

has adopted a self-promotion policy. Each promotion cycle, Googlers are asked to put themselves up for promotions. Unfortunately, management was finding that women specifically just weren't doing that. So instead of shrugging their shoulders and assuming women were just less ambitious than men, they tested out a thought experiment.

Each promotion cycle, Alan Eustace, one of their Heads of Engineering, would send out an email to let everyone know that promotion applications were due. When they did that one small thing, women's applications for promotion skyrocketed. If Eustace forgot to send the email, the number of women promotions would fall off a cliff.

"The data was clear," Laszlo Bock said.[121] "If we tried to have a small nudge by simply presenting information, it could fix part of the problem. We prefer this to a bureaucratic top-down approach."

Why weren't women putting themselves up for promotion? Well, it's kind of a double-edged sword. All values that would be good leadership qualities if we were discussing a man are exactly the qualities we often penalize women for. If a man speaks up for himself, he's assertive. If a woman speaks up for herself, she's bossy. In fact, I was recently talking to a female founder who was pitching to a VC, and she told me that an overly casual Silicon Valley bro had called her "bossy." She tried to shrug it off, but it threw her off her game for the rest of the pitch. She was so angry at herself later both for not having said anything to him at the time and also for letting him shake her. "I can't believe I didn't say anything," she said. "I run a company, and I let this little fool put me in the corner." That's how it is for people who aren't white men. Stereotype threat is a real thing, and it has huge impacts for nonwhite, nonmen in tech. In order to be an ally and advocate, we need to understand these

---

121 Cecilia Kang, "Google Data-Mines Its Approach to Promoting Women," *Washington Post*, April 2, 2014, https://www.washingtonpost.com/news/the-switch/wp/2014/04/02/google-data-mines-its-women-problem/.

terms and their impact. And we need the other allies in the room to say, "Dude, no."

TL;DR:

- Hire for great teams, not just stars. Studies across multiple industries prove stars are only stars on their home team.
- Build teams for charismatic interactions within and without the team for success; psychological safety is a crucial factor in successful teams.
- Personality tests like DiSC are great tools, as long as there's room made for cultural diversity and individual differences that a lot of times these tests don't account for.
- Some conflict can actually be productive when managed by an effective leader and not just swept under the rug.
- If you need to use NDAs, make sure that their impact is to protect trade secrets and not to silence employees who are being victimized or oppressed.
- Use data to track performance, not biases and assumptions.
- Recognize how much biases may already be impacting the career trajectory of marginalized team members, and manage against that.

PART 3

DIVERSITY, EQUITY, AND INCLUSION AT WORK

In January 2019, Sallie Krawcheck, CEO and Cofounder of Ellevest and longtime "senior woman on Wall Street," appeared on *The Daily Show* with Trevor Noah to discuss diversity and the gender pay gap. Here's how it went.

Trevor Noah: *It's good to have you here, especially in this time. It feels like businesses are in the news for how they are handling moving into a space where women are included. The gender pay gap is a large conversation that we are having. As a whole, it feels like the world is moving in the right direction.* [Sallie Krawcheck grimaces, shakes her head.] *As someone who has been a CEO, though, do you agree with that?*

Sallie Krawcheck: *No! As someone who is a person, I don't...and a woman. It's not happening. The gender pay gap, which is decades away from closing for white women, a hundred-plus years away from closing for Black women, two hundred-plus years away from closing for Latina women.*

Trevor Noah: *Wow.*

Sallie Krawcheck: *Right?! The number of female CEOs in the Fortune 500 has declined by 25%. We're not making any progress. We're not moving forward. And this is despite the fact there is reams of research out there, Trevor, that says that, you know, as a capitalist society, we look for better returns, and "The greater diversity at the top of these companies can lead to better returns, higher profitability, greater innovation, etc." And we are going sideways at best, and in many cases backward.*

Trevor Noah: *So, you were a CEO of Smith Barney, uh, Merrill Lynch Wealth Management...when you were in those positions, what did you notice from the top? Is there something that happens maybe, when you're a CEO, where you're like, "Oh, I can't help the ladies," or like is there a roadblock that is an institutional thing?*

Sallie Krawcheck (jokingly, as a male CEO): *Well, you know, The Pipeline! We've got our diversity committee! And we've got our mentoring program! And, you know, but we need to let our managers manage!*

[continues, as herself]

And so I think CEOs really do believe in the power of diversity, but middle management is where diversity goes to die, because when it comes time to promoting the next person and you say, "Well, I think I read some research one time about diversity drives better results, but that young man, that young man that reminds me so darn much of myself when I was younger, I just feel like he's going to do a better job."

Trevor Noah: *That's a powerful way to put it because you read so many times about how, uh, people hire the people who remind them most of themselves. And so, you have a vicious cycle of these men, who are white, hiring white men who remind them of themselves and sometimes it's an implicit bias, but you've come out and said that you don't believe that bias training helps.*

(Sallie Krawcheck shakes her head.)

Trevor Noah: *You don't believe that these "diversity programs" help.*

Sallie Krawcheck: *Why don't we just say that everything we're doing doesn't help? Right? If we're not moving forward, then what we're doing isn't working.*

Trevor Noah: *What do you think would help?*

Sallie Krawcheck: *I think CEOs deciding that it will be done and having it be done and overruling their managers who aren't getting it done and really paying them for it. That's what works. Marc Benioff at Salesforce saying, "I'm, you know, forget about the reasons we're paying this person less, this woman less, this white guy, and this person of color, we're just closing these gender pay gaps" and just doing it, is what makes the difference.*

Trevor Noah: *Let me ask you this, then: The argument that you hear a lot of CEOs say or middle managers or anything, they always come back with the same thing. They say, "Well, Sallie, I want to give these people promotions, but, I mean, I don't just want to give the job to someone 'cause she's a woman. You know..."*

Sallie Krawcheck interjects, joking, as a male CEO: *"We can't lower our standards!"*

(They riff on this, audience cheers.)

Trevor Noah: *Yeah, but how do you answer when they say, "We don't want to lower our standards?"*

Sallie Krawcheck: *Well, let's go back to the research. You and I have talked about this before. The research shows that we're not lowering our standards in business in order to promote women and people of color; we actually hold them to a higher standard. That white men are promoted based on potential—"I think that young man is going places, let's give him a chance,"—whereas women and people of color are promoted based on what they've achieved. So when you hear, gentlemen, when you hear your spouse, your friends, etc. come home and say, "Gosh, I have to work twice as hard to make it, you know, as far," there really is some truth to this. And again, I think it's because of these implicit—I don't know if we want to use the word* bias—*but this comfort level we have with bringing along people like ourselves.*[122]

---

122 Trevor Noah, "Sallie Krawcheck - How Ellevest Is Challenging the Gender Investing Gap | the Daily Show," *The Daily Show with Trevor Noah*, February 5,

This example has always been one of my favorites, not only because I'm a big fan of Sallie's but also because it covers what I hear most often with a little more humor than I typically hear it delivered. Sallie Krawcheck, it goes without saying, has fought through more than her fair share of bias (often overt) during her career on Wall Street, and to this day leads and supports programs for diversity, especially for women in finance and across other industries.

A good judge of diversity at the top of companies has always been the S&P 500. Who runs the 500 companies that make the most money year after year in a capitalist society has always been a bellwether for how leadership sees itself on the big stage and how much diversity is represented there. As Marian Wright Edelman said, "You can't be what you can't see." This year, we have a new record high: 38 women are running top companies, up from 33 last year. For comparison, 20 years ago, there were 2. But that still leaves a lot to be desired when it comes to diversity for women at the top. There have only ever been two Black women CEOs in the Fortune 500: Ursula Burns of Xerox (who is, in fact, Afro-Latina, and stepped down in 2016) and Mary Winston, who was interim CEO of Bed Bath & Beyond for six months in 2019. That same year, when Geisha Williams of PG&E stepped down, there were no longer any Black or Latina female CEOs in the Fortune 500.[123] This list is obviously ever-changing, but it's where we are now.

Women and people of color are graduating from top universities at greater numbers than men for the first time in history. Women make up more than half of the U.S. population and yet fluctuate on average between holding 5–6% of the CEO positions. And to be clear, every one of these CEOs is a white woman.

2019, YouTube video, 9:32, https://www.youtube.com/watch?v=mdxS8S_06VM.

123 Emma Hinchliffe, "The Number of Women Running Fortune 500 Companies Hits an All-Time Record," *Fortune*, May 18, 2020, https://fortune.com/2020/05/18/women-ceos-fortune-500-2020/.

What's happening here?

As Sallie Krawcheck half-jokingly refrains: "It's the pipeline!"

Sadly, I hear that more than I don't, and whether the bias is intentional or not, it's the excuse people in positions capable of making change use to give up the fight. The following chapters are all about why you shouldn't let this harmful narrative sway you from your allyship goals.

Chapter 8

HANDLING DAY-TO-DAY OPERATIONS

A few weeks ago, I sat down for Zoom coffee and gossip with a friend who is an antiracist educator for nonprofit organizations and other businesses. We were commiserating about how often when you consult, you hear the same fictive narrative from company to company. For her, there's this false idea that NPOs are gentler and care more about their employees than other companies, like tech companies, do. Through our conversation, I was able to convince her nothing could be further from the truth. As much as I fight with tech leaders, it comes from a place of knowing that they value the best proven strategies and how much they want to be the best at everything contributes positively to my work.

Tech companies usually don't tell me we have to make progress slowly—if it's not working today, it needs to be fixed tomorrow. I do well in that space because I'm not good at waiting. She was surprised and talked about how in NPOs with multiple chapters or locations, there's a common pattern URGs often experience. Employees would have a bad experience in one particular branch of an organization, gaslit into thinking it was probably their fault and individual to that person.

Finally, because they're nonprofits, the leaders (while making real money) can convince everyone else to work for less because the work is so important, an experience that sounded *very* familiar to me from my super brief time in the world of nonprofits.

We went on for a while commiserating about our shared experiences, and then I shared a refrain that I hear often: "How about, 'We care about diversity but…'"

"You mean, 'We care about diversity, but it's not our only priority?'" she countered.

"No, it's always, 'We care about diversity, but we don't want to lower our standards,'" I said.

She looked at me as though I had grown a second head.

At that moment, I realized what had happened.

"Do they really say that to you?" she said.

"Yes, almost every single time," I answered honestly.

I looked at her perfect brown skin and radiant smile, which had faltered only slightly. "They don't say that to you, do they?" I asked.

She shook her head. "No, I'm Black, so I guess they know better than to tell me the real reasons behind their nonsense."

"I'm sorry," I said. "I didn't even realize."

"No, don't be sorry," she said with an even bigger smile. "If they're comfortable telling you what's up, that means you can make changes. You can fix things. You can make things better."

"I am," I said. "I will."

"I know it," she said.

The 5 Big Arguments

When people ask me about DEI and try to convince me how committed to diversity they are as a company, they always argue the same five issues:

- We know diversity is important, but we don't want to lower our standards.
- There just aren't qualified women, people of color, or LGBTQ+ identifying candidates applying to our open positions. (I hear this especially often in STEM fields.)
- We have a mentorship program in place, but we're still not seeing women and people of color getting promoted.
- It's true we see fewer women and people of color or LGBTQ+ identifying employees at the top of the organization, but there are unbiased reasons for that. Maybe women are less ambitious than men because they have babies.[124]
- Are you saying we should have quotas?!

On that last point, I'm not saying anyone should have a quota. In fact, we happen to know that diversity quotas can have serious consequences when diversity is viewed as a box to check off.

Anecdotally, if you're interested in ways that "diversity quotas" can backfire, Susan Fowler, author of *Whistleblower: My Journey to Silicon Valley and Fight for Justice at Uber*, tells a particularly harrowing story about how her manager would write bad reviews for her and other team members who were women or people of color so they couldn't transfer off his team. By blocking the career growth of his direct reports, he was keeping his diversity "quota" up—something he bragged about to other male managers.

Last year, Facebook announced it had started assessing how managers address diversity and inclusion in their bi-annual performance reviews.[125] While the announcement was shared around social media as

---

124 This isn't a joke. I hear the "babies" argument all the time.
125 Salvador Rodriguez, "Facebook Ties Improving Employee Diversity to Executive Performance Reviews," CNBC, July 16, 2020, https://www.cnbc.com/2020/07/16/facebook-will-evaluate-execs-on-diversity-inclusion-maxine-williams.html.

big tech taking its inclusion and allyship responsibilities seriously, I felt hesitant. I wondered if this same time next year, we'd be hearing about terrible ways that requirement became weaponized against the people it was intended to include. Maybe I'm just being negative, but I'm ready and willing to be proved wrong.

Pinterest, another big player in tech, is still currently facing its own skeletons in the closet about racial bias within the organization. At the end of May 2020, Ifeoma Ozoma and Aerica Shimizu Banks (two Black, female employees), quit together. They cited Pinterest's outward support for Black Lives Matter not being the same as their internal support practices for Black lives as their reason for leaving.

According to the *Washington Post*: "The two women and other former employees, who were inspired to speak after they saw the [BLM support] Twitter threads, say there is little accountability at Pinterest, where some subordinates were berated, women were pushed out without warning, and executives in Silbermann's [Ben Silbermann, CEO] inner circle faced no consequences despite repeated complaints."[126]

In the midst of this, Pinterest was scrambling to fix its toxic culture problems by hiring DEI specialists, and even the job descriptions for those positions weren't reflecting best practices. I know this because DEI specialists in my network were sharing them with each other and critiquing them.

"Immediately I recognized problems. First, important decisions were often made in sidebar conversations between Ben and two or three of his lieutenants, invariably men, who often did not have complete information. These decisions were difficult to track and

---

126 Nitasha Tiku, "Black Women Say Pinterest Created a Den of Discrimination— Despite Its Image as the Nicest Company in Tech," *Washington Post*, July 4, 2020, https://www.washingtonpost.com/technology/2020/07/03/pinterest-race-bias-black-employees/.

their illogic was often demoralizing to the people who understood the issues better.

Ben appeared to listen to only a few people and sealed himself off from opposing viewpoints. Ben's "in-group," the men invited to the "meeting after the meeting," held all the power and influence. This structure was detrimental to Pinterest's culture, velocity, and results. The senior management team was driven by backstabbing and gossip as executives competed for Ben's attention.

A colleague once remarked, "The only way we get things done here is hiding things." Day-to-day operations were marked by secretiveness. Executive meetings were brisk, formal, and did not confront critical issues the company faced. There was both no collegial banter and no debate. This made it difficult for me to create the culture I believe is most effective.

Several times in my career, I have been told that I am excessively transparent. When everything is out in the open, it makes workplaces fairer, happier, and more effective. I knew that I could not foster a better culture unless our people could get to know and trust one another, so I organized off-sites, mixing hiking, drawing, and cooking with serious topics. In a short time, we achieved a sense of trust and clarity.

My team told me they enjoyed my direct style and bad grammar. (I am French, and English is my second language.) I loved working with them. I put in place a series of processes designed to foster communication and cooperation, including Objectives and Key Results, a popular goal-setting strategy in Silicon Valley. I asked each of my direct reports to send me a summary of their highlights and lowlights from the week, as well as their plan for the next week. I read them all and sent summaries to the entire organization, so everyone knew everyone else's priorities and challenges.

Soon Pinterest started making decisions faster. We launched our product in international markets and opened sales offices across Europe. Our sales process, customer segmentation, and overall pipeline metrics became more disciplined. I brought in phenomenal talent in marketing and business development. Our communications team focused more on external rather than internal audiences, defining Pinterest and telling our story to the world. We were on the path to an IPO.

When the founders redrafted Pinterest's mission in early 2019, one of the five values was "care with candor." I interpreted this initiative as a commitment to changing the culture. Team members would now be encouraged to share their ideas directly and respectfully. Employees who had been excluded would finally have a voice. Ben asked me to be the company spokesperson for the "care with candor" value. I did not seem to understand what everyone else knew intuitively: saying what you really thought was still dangerous at Pinterest. I was naively proud.

On the morning Pinterest announced this new mission, the entire workforce gathered in San Francisco's Orpheum Theater. I stood onstage and explained how important it was for Pinterest to foster transparency and direct feedback. My message echoed around the grand theater but fell on deaf ears.[127] *"*

—**Francoise Brougher**, former COO at Pinterest

I don't mean to drag Pinterest specifically—there are many examples of how thinking of diversity as a box to check or a quota to fill would have the opposite effect. Team members who weren't interested in having implicit bias training or diversity guidelines in the first place can point

---

127 Francoise Brougher, "The Pinterest Paradox: Cupcakes and Toxicity," Medium, August 11, 2020, https://medium.com/digital-diplomacy/the-pinterest-paradox-cupcakes-and-toxicity-57ed6bd76960.

to the negative outcomes and say, "See? I'm not racist! This just doesn't work." Following the letter of the law and not the spirit never works. Allyship training for managers and executives, on the other hand? That's what has shown actual promise because it inspires more understanding and empathy that leads to action.

I'm not here for the letter of the law. I don't do this work for compliance as there are plenty of books and trainings on that. I'm here for the spirit. If you want to do actual good, if you want to ally up and get actual results because you believe in the work and care about inclusion, that's a good enough place to start.

There are multiple levels of awareness when it comes to diversity, equity, and inclusion in America today. Starting with those of you who received this book as a gift from a person belonging to a URG who has "adopted" you; we'll call you "Curious Caucasians." You want to be a better ally, and that's totally cool—I'm here to support you. Thanks for reading this far!

But there's another kind of person I can't help. Let's call him "Todd."[128] Todd doesn't want to be inspired. Todd wants to argue about how he's not a racist. You know at least one Todd, and he doesn't change. Todd prefers to simply watch Dwayne "The Rock" Johnson's workouts without putting in any of the work, and he likely complains about how Dwayne's doing it.

Fun fact about how just a tiny bit of bias affects outcomes for women and URGs at the top of companies: a study was published in *American Psychology* in 1996, whereby a computer simulation was written to test what a 1% bias against women in performance reviews would have over time in a company.[129] The "company" has eight levels

---

128 Sorry to nice guys named Todd, including my own friend Todd. I chose this name for the *Scrubs* character.

129 Richard F. Martell, David M. Lane, and Cynthia Emrich, "Male-Female Differences: A Computer Simulation.," *American Psychologist* 51, no. 2 (February 1996): 157–58, https://doi.org/10.1037/0003-066x.51.2.157.

(entry to C-Suite), and when the program begins, each level is 50% men and 50% women. Each level has 15% attrition, and the simulation filled positions by pulling somebody up from one of the lower levels. The simulation chose each "person" based on their randomly generated performance score. But remember, with a 1% bias against women. The simulation is run until every original person from the company is gone and replaced by someone new, and the lowest level is always replaced by 50%. The simulation was run 20 times, and then results were averaged. A 1% bias against women led to the C-Suite being 35% women and 65% men. Which is what we see in most organizations today.

Amplification

In 2016, a story came out[130] about the Obama White House and how women and nonbinary folks were fighting to make themselves heard in the sea of men. When they first joined the team, many female+ staffers reported feeling like outsiders and struggling to break in. As time went on, they banded together and developed an in-meeting strategy of "amplification." Basically, when a female+ staffer had an idea, women+ in the room would repeat the idea and give credit to its author. This had two benefits: firstly, it forced the men at the table to notice their contributions, and secondly, it kept men in the room from taking credit for their ideas.[131]

Things got much better for female+ staffers by Obama's second term. Eventually, more female and nonbinary staffers headed up departments and, according to senior advisor Valerie Jarrett: "I think having a critical

---

130 Emily Crockett, "The Amazing Tool That Women in the White House Used to Fight Gender Bias," *Vox*, September 14, 2016, https://www.vox.com/2016/9/14/12914370/white-house-obama-women-gender-bias-amplification.

131 Also known as "he-peating," when a man takes credit for an idea a woman and/or person from a URG has and claims it as his own. Yep, it's so common there's a word for that.

mass makes a difference. It's fair to say that there was a lot of testosterone flowing in those early days."[132]

The important takeaway from this example is that even on teams where you would assume no one is out to be discriminatory or leave anyone's voice out, that is still exactly what happens. We've inherited these workplaces for the most part, and even for new companies, there are deeply rooted oppressive and discriminatory systems in our fields. If you aren't tripping over it every day, which is to say if it isn't holding you back personally, you might not notice it for other people.

There are a lot of ways day to day to be the voice of allyship for women and URGs in meetings, in offices, and behind closed doors. The "amplification" meeting example is one of many.

According to Sarah Bedrick from Compt, reflecting on her time at HubSpot, she remembers exactly when her career started to get more traction. Brian Halligan, CEO of HubSpot, found out they were both in Toastmasters[133] and started asking her to sit in on his keynote practices. She'd offer insight, and over time, he started recommending her for stretch assignments or asking her opinion in front of others at meetings. This is textbook sponsorship and allyship, and we know it works.

Sponsoring Coworkers

As Karen Catlin writes on the Better Allies forum of Medium,[134] DEI in day-to-day operations includes getting to know coworkers from

---

132 Claire Landsbaum, "Obama's Female Staffers Came up with a Genius Strategy to Make Sure Their Voices Were Heard," The Cut (September 13, 2016), https://www.thecut.com/2016/09/heres-how-obamas-female-staffers-made-their-voices-heard.html.

133 "Toastmasters International - Home," Toastmasters.org, accessed January 27, 2021, https://www.toastmasters.org/.

134 Better Allies®, "5 Things Allies Can Do to Sponsor Coworkers from Underrepresented Groups," Medium, May 22, 2020, https://medium.com/@betterallies/5-things-allies-can-do-to-sponsor-coworkers-from-underrepresented-groups-266cd512e289.

underrepresented groups so we can speak about them and their work when they're not around. Catlin recommends five things allies can do to sponsor coworkers from underrepresented groups:

- Speak their name when they aren't around.
- Endorse them publicly.
- Invite them to high-profile meetings.
- Share their career goals with decision-makers.
- Recommend them for stretch assignments and speaking opportunities.

TL;DR:

- When I consult privately, I regularly hear some version of "Of course diversity is a priority, but…"
- I don't agree with quotas. I think quotas lead to people engaging in their worst impulses. I do agree with representative workplaces.
- Don't *only* try to hire more-diverse workforces to prove you care about diversity. Work on the inclusiveness of your culture so the people you hire don't immediately have terrible experiences with you and leave.
- Because of workplace toxicity issues, including racism and misogyny, we're seeing companies like Pinterest having to face their skeletons in the closet. They aren't the first, and they definitely won't be the last.
- No amount of performative allyship will positively impact a toxic workplace. Do the real work, or expect that nothing will change and watch it go badly for your bottom line.
- Bias has enormous impact. As little as a 1% bias against women can lead to the skewed representation we see at the top of companies today.

- There are many proven ways of being more effective allies in the workplace. I've included examples from many organizations here.

Chapter 9
TRUSTING TEAM MEMBERS

J anis Middleton is the SVP, Executive Director of Multicultural and Inclusion Strategy at Guided by Good, an Atlanta-based creative company focused on DEI at the forefront of its culture. Guided by Good operates Trade School, a holistic content shop that helps clients accelerate and scale the creation of high-quality, effective content, Dendro, an independent consultancy working upstream with clients to fill the gap between where management consultants leave off and creative agencies begin, and 22squared, an advertising agency. When she first started working with the company 2013, starting with 22squared, the picture was a little bit different. "I felt like I wasn't really being seen when it came to promotions and recognition," says Janis, whose life had been changed by the Trayvon Martin killing; she was fully committed to DEI at the workplace "My resume was growing, but my title wasn't, my paycheck wasn't—the things that usually come with working hard just weren't happening for me." Her managers understood, she says, and understood there was an absence of DEI within the company culture.

Janis left for another agency—until she received a call from 22Squared telling her they had hired a diversity trainer who was coming in to hold focus groups and share the results transparently. One of her must-haves for returning to 22Squared was knowing the company was taking DEI steps.

"Fairness has always been my purpose in life," says Janis, who soon became a trusted team member who could make DEI work. "The first time around, I allowed someone else to control my destiny. This time around, I wanted to be at the helm to ensure the right thing would be done for marginalized people in the industry. And I cannot believe the agency I work for at this point."

Janis and 22Squared began hosting "Netflix and Chat," where people would watch an appointed TV show, documentary, movie, etc., and employees would gather a few weeks later to discuss the material. The first was Ava DuVernay's *13th*, which was "an eye-opener," she says. "The response in the room was so refreshing because people were open and honest. So we started doing more documentaries on marriage equality, our Hispanic brothers and sisters, our Asian brothers and sisters. This has really worked in our favor to open up courageous conversations."

Soon, the agency was following Dr. Martin Luther King's "Sunday Suppers," where people with various views, even opposing ones, could come together and discuss current events. Now, Janis has presented an action plan that ladders up to three aspects of DEI as it influences culture. "Culture is inside of our walls, right?" she says. "That's the hiring, the recruiting on the ground, and making sure we are having real and authentic conversations and are creating an inclusive environment."

Next are the clients. Janis acts as a strategist, helping clients adjust to shifts such as Black Lives Matter and COVID-19 and ensuring messaging stays on the DEI track.

Janis is keeping 22Squared accountable to itself, measuring the impact of its efforts and continuing to push collectively for change. After the George Floyd killing, for example, they had 180 attendees at an internal "Brave Space" event. Says Janis: "Our allies were there too, and it was beautiful to see and hear Black voices amplified and our allies being right there to listen."

Building Trust through Feedback

Let's shift from Janis's story to how feedback builds trust. Why do we view positive feedback suspiciously? Meanwhile, we spread negative feedback liberally through "radical honesty."

I'm all for honesty, as I see how it builds authenticity on teams, but I'm also proscience when it comes to how people respond to feedback. According to Frances Frei and Anne Morriss in *Unleashed*, positive and negative feedback should be delivered at a ratio of 5:1. So for every time you correct someone's work or behavior, you need to have also found five other times to offer praise. The feedback should be public (when possible), immediate, and specific.[135]

Call-Out vs. Call-In

We're living in a "call-out culture." If you see something racist, homophobic, transphobic, misogynistic, or xenophobic, it's your responsibility to call it out. I'm a big fan of the call-out and have been *checked* many times over my life. This means I've been publicly and privately corrected for being wrong about something cultural or social. Anyone who has gotten to any level of allyship has been checked. It's good for me. It builds character and forces me to be uncomfortable and learn, especially if *there is no shame attached.* You'll be checked on your allyship journey as well, so keep in mind that how you respond to being checked will set the tone for how others view you. Be humble, open, and honest—your peers and direct reports will be inspired by your leadership and will want to follow your example.

---

135 Frances Frei and Anne Morriss, *Unleashed: The Unapologetic Leader's Guide to Empowering Everyone around You* (Boston, MA: Harvard Business Review Press, 2020).

Many people in call-out culture "spill the tea" about it on social media, regularly using #ThatsTheTea. Spilling the tea, pouring the tea, it just means to tell the truth, especially if it's a hard truth that people might not want to hear. Which people? Well, white people. White people don't like to be called out for being wrong about something and generalized about—especially when we're talking about racism. White folks don't like to be lumped together, and they will work hard to distance themselves from "other white people." This is especially true of progressives, who will cite numerous reasons why they can't be racist even if they've said something clearly racist. For the white people reading this—disbelieving someone's experience because it is uncomfortable for you to hear it or think about it removes their agency. You are making them invisible and doubting their integrity to the community at large, and you are silencing them for your comfort. Be humble and listen—it's the least you can do from your position of privilege.

Call-out culture is great for public issues—public companies, celebrities, public personas, social media, etc. But what I'd like to argue for is something known as "call-in culture." According to The Consent Crew, a call-in is when you talk with someone privately about their behavior (or you wait to talk in person), and it is considered a less incendiary route to work through conflict.[136] If you're thinking that I'm tone policing[137] here, I'm not.

Stay with me on this. I believe, as others do, that in a work or professional setting, calling someone in privately to tell them how their actions or their words are offensive or demeaning can do a lot

136 Mel Mariposa Cassidy, "A Practical Guide to Calling In," The Consent Crew, May 29, 2016, https://theconsentcrew.org/2016/05/29/calling-in/.
137 Tess Martin, "Racism 101: Tone Policing," Medium, January 12, 2018, https://medium.com/@tessintrovert/racism-101-tone-policing-92481c044b6a. Tone policing is a diversion strategy where a person with no real defense will take issue with the passion with which you express your argument (policing) rather than the argument itself because your emotions about oppression make them uncomfortable.

of good. It can educate that person, maybe leading them toward a path of enlightenment, and it has the additional bonus of not starting a public bridge-burning blaze that takes you down with it. Use real recent examples, and don't wait and use general terms such as, "Sophie, sometimes the things you say are kind of racist." Sophie doesn't believe you, and she's already on the phone to HR.

Instead, immediately after the offense has occurred, step into Sophie's office and say: "Hey, Sophie, just wanted to let you know when you said that 'all Asians are cheap,' even though you are married to an Asian man, that's still problematic for people who hear it, and it perpetuates stereotypes that dehumanize Asian people. I thought you might want to hear it from someone who knows that wasn't your intent."[138]

Do I think Sophie is going to be psyched? No. Do I know that it's better than calling her out publicly in a meeting? Yes. If, on the other hand, Sophie has been spoken to multiple times about these issues privately and is due for a public check, then by all means speak up. I support call-outs under the right circumstances. We've all gotten a good call-out and lived; it's how we become better allies. If Sophie is a white woman, don't @ me; just write it down for your exit interview.

Believe People

If someone comes to you to report that an employee is being racist, misogynistic, homophobic, transphobic, or other types of abusive, or the most uncomfortable option: you yourself have offended them, then take a beat.

You don't need to know everything, and you don't have to be right all the time. Allyship is a learning process. The effort and willingness to learn and be wrong is what makes you an effective leader, and no one has a PhD for each culture and ethnicity in existence and is doing

---

138 This is a true story, by the way.

everything right all the time. We're all working together. That said, if someone comes to you about you or someone else, believe them. Act as if what they are saying is absolutely true until proven otherwise. Understand what it would take for someone to come to a person in power and ask for help. If they've come to you, you are trusted. You have integrity. This is your allyship moment. How will you handle it? I suggest you believe them, establish open lines of communication, and do not try to minimize or sweep things under the rug. Work together to make it right, and make it right for real.[139]

Every Woman Is Dwayne "The Rock" Johnson

Sometimes when I talk to men in tech, there's a familiar refrain that it's "every man's worst nightmare" to be accused of sexual harassment at work. And "I don't even know how to talk to women anymore, after this '#MeToo' stuff." On behalf of all women+: please stop saying this. Don't complain to us that before, it was okay to sexually harass women, and now it isn't; who raised you?

So now that we've got that out of the way, I'd like to invoke my future friend Dwayne "The Rock" Johnson,[140] with a fun way to remember how to treat women+ in the workplace: Treat every woman on your team as if she were Dwayne "The Rock" Johnson.[141] Should you ask the hot new "The Rock" intern out for drinks that he doesn't feel comfortable declining because his job might be at stake? Nope. Should you compliment The Rock on how his T-shirt fits today? Probably not. Should you ask The Rock to order the birthday cake for Ted's birthday

---

139 I give more examples on how in the next chapter on trust, and I also teach online classes.

140 And Mr. Johnson, if you ever see this, I'm available seven days a week for coffee, and my kids loved you in *Moana*.

141 Anne Victoria Clark, "The Rock Test: A Hack for Men Who Don't Want to Be Accused of Sexual Harassment," Medium, October 9, 2019, https://humanparts. medium.com/the-rock-test-a-hack-for-men-who-dont-want-to-be-accused-of-sexual-harassment-73c45e0b49af.

even though you didn't ask anyone else whose job that might be? I wouldn't. Should you text The Rock flirty messages about your "open" relationship? That seems like it would have a bad outcome. See? Easy test. Now you understand boundaries. Every woman is The Rock.

Building Trust on Teams

Trust is more crucial than ever to team building. As I have noted before, psychological safety is the number one predictor of successful teams, and psychological safety comes from trust. How do we build trust through the lens of diversity and inclusion? Firstly, by establishing certain common ground. People are largely driven by the same needs and goals across cultures. On teams, this can be even more true because we are all striving toward the same goals, and that's where strong leadership comes in.

When I talk to more-marginalized members of teams, I'm often met with concerns about sharing the same goals as the rest of the team while feeling less comfortable expressing a viewpoint that may not be shared by the majority. I'll give you an example: I had an interviewee (let's call her Kayla) who was at the top of her field in finance. She felt like her CEO really understood her. She felt like he was aware of the needs of the URGs under his leadership, and he was continuously learning how to lead authentically. Kayla trusted him. One day, in a client meeting where she was the only woman at the table, and similarly the only Asian person in the room, her boss turned to her and said, "Let's make sure we open the kimono on that deal."

She recalls that meeting with shame and disappointment. "I felt my cheeks redden. My mouth dried out, and I was suddenly very aware of being the only person like me in the room," says Kayla. "When I looked at everyone else, they were nodding and smiling as if he had said something funny. Or because saying it to me had made it funny. But I didn't speak for the rest of the meeting, and I felt like him not knowing that was racist was maybe worse, but it definitely shook my trust in thinking he was my ally." Kayla didn't tell her boss that what he had said made her feel that way. Because when a person of an underrepresented identity brings up an incident of accidental racism, the offending party almost never receives that information with grace. They don't say, "Oh my gosh, I didn't even realize. Thank you for that feedback. I am always looking to do better." In fact, they say, "Oh, you know what I meant. You can't say anything to anyone anymore—don't be so sensitive!"

Everyone else in that room had an opportunity to be an ally for Kayla and, unfortunately, they failed her just as much as her boss did. It cannot be the responsibility of any member of a URG to speak up against these sorts of behaviors alone, or else they will see similar pushback and defensiveness from the offending party.

A survey by EY released in 2016 found that less than half of survey respondents globally had trust in their employer. In the U.S., it's 38%.[142]

For respondents aged 19–68, the top reasons for lack of trust in one's employer were compensation related: "equal opportunity for pay and promotion" paired with "lack of strong leadership," "too much employee turnover," and "not fostering a collaborative work environment." These are all inclusion related.

In the same survey, the leading determinants in having trust were: "delivers on promises" (67%); "provides job security" (64%); "provides fair compensation and good benefits" (63%); and "communicates openly/transparently" (59%). Lastly, there was a tie for fifth place between "provides equal opportunity for pay and promotion for all people regardless of differences" and "operates ethically" (57%).

---

142 Ernst & Young, "EY Research Reveals Less than Half of Full-Time Workers Surveyed Globally Trust Their Employer, Boss or Colleagues a Great Deal," www. prnewswire.com, June 21, 2016, https://www.prnewswire.com/news-releases/ey-research-reveals-less-than-half-of-full-time-workers-surveyed-globally-trust-their-employer-boss-or-colleagues-a-great-deal-300287869.html.

When you break women+ out of that study and ask what is the most important factor to influence trust in your employer, EY found that women+ by and large said, it is "pay and promotion equity." For women + in Gen Z, that was (86%); Millennials (70%); Gen Xers (73%); and Boomers (81%).

How Do You Build Trust?

1. You lead by example: Leading a team is just like being a parent. "Do as I say, not as I do" just doesn't work here. You need to model what it looks like to be authentic, and if you don't know the answer to something, ask in the meeting so others can see you being vulnerable.

2. Give trust: You want people to trust you? You need to trust them. Show your team you respect and trust them by giving them the power to make decisions on their own. Decentralize decision-making authority. You aren't going to be looking over their shoulder every day; explain that this is because you trust them.

3. Communicate: If I could have you take away one thing from this book, it would be to communicate with your team. I worked for someone in my younger days who would respond to email questions I had about his team with pithy one-liners about actual interpersonal issues. I'd write lengthy emails with the facts, my assumptions, and my plan for solutions for him to deal with it effectively, and he'd write back "Not good." Now, he was busy; I understood that. But prioritizing your people is a great way to get less busy.

4. Empathize: Someone on my team came to me in tears because she felt like her mentor just didn't care about her. When I flagged this for his attention, he told me she was "too sensitive." Another time, I was speaking with the CEO, and he told me he

loved "hiring women." When I brought this up the next day as a positive to my direct boss, he said, "Yeah, Di, he loves to hire women because he can pay you less; don't give him too much credit." Before saying or thinking something, try to put yourself in that person's shoes. Before saying something to someone else that might get back to them, try to imagine how that might feel; and for goodness's sake, before sending texts and emails, always try to imagine what they will sound like read aloud in court by a grumpy attorney.

5. Get to know each other: The easiest way for people to trust you is to let them get to know you authentically. Do your team-building work by participating in lunches and get-togethers during work hours. Don't put yourself behind a closed door and hope that your actions will speak for themselves because they won't. People see you through their own lens, and you need to speak for yourself.

Remote Teams

Now that we're in the middle of a global pandemic, I think we've recognized how much remote work can have a positive impact on our lives. That being said, it's certainly making it harder to build trust and authenticity on teams. Here are some pointers for building trust on remote teams:

1. Have smaller meetings: 1:1s are the best, and if you can't do that, smaller groups work just fine. If someone hasn't had a chance to speak on a video call, make sure to include that person by asking for their input.

2. Meet face to face: Slack and other chats are great, but nothing beats having an opportunity to look at another human while you work on a problem together. It builds trust as well as empathy.

3. Get over it: People have kids, dogs, lives, whatever. If it isn't affecting their work, it isn't an issue for you. Empathize with their situation, support them, and move on. Because if I have to apologize for my kids existing one more time because someone thinks they're going to evaporate during business hours, I may lose my mind. If you can't think of anything supportive to say, try, "No need to apologize; we're all in this together," or just smile with encouragement.

4. Have remote activities: We're trying a million remote activities on my team, and it's not just to boost morale, it's also to build trust and let people who work in three different time zones to have an opportunity to get to know one another outside the context of who they have to interact with to get work done. There are lists. The most successful teams get half of their information and interactions from people outside their immediate work group.

5. Facilitate: If you're a leader, and someone isn't speaking in a group call, find something you need to ask them about[143]—and ask them in front of the group. If you're on a social call, ask that person how something that's going on in their life is going. In order to do that, you need to know what those things are. If you don't have the time to know everyone, and you have an admin, ask your admin—they have to know everyone and everything...they are your facilitators.

TL;DR:

• Survey your team by holding focus groups. Use your inclusion team to track your progress, and share with everyone your findings and plans to do better.

---

143 Within reason: don't out personal issues they haven't shared, of course.

- Every time you need to correct someone on your team, you need to praise them five times as often. Praise should be as specific and public as possible.
- There are a lot of great benefits to practicing call-ins in the workplace.
- Treat every woman at work as if she is Dwayne "The Rock" Johnson.
- In the U.S., 36% of employees have trust in their employers. Build trust by establishing common ground and common goals.
- Trust is crucial to team success.

Chapter 10

LEADING BY EXAMPLE

When you talk to executives about hiring strategies for tech start-ups, the advice is pretty much the same: you need to be able to spot the diamond in the rough because folks who have had traditional career paths are already on the radar of the bigger companies, and they'll outbid you every time. It's a skill to be able to recruit good talent under those conditions.

I decided to join an early-stage start-up pretty recently even though I normally prefer my consultant lifestyle because I had never found a company that I felt like I could invest in. It turns out, many of us with intersecting and/or underrepresented identities tend to enjoy working for ourselves because we don't feel like we'll ever find a home that's inclusive and supports us as we are. Millennials represent a 50% majority in the workforce today.[144] Millennials care about authenticity more than any generation before us, and according to a recent study by LinkedIn,

---

144 Richard Fry, "Millennials Are the Largest Generation in the U.S. Labor Force," Pew Research Center (Pew Research Center, April 11, 2018), https://www. pewresearch.org/fact-tank/2018/04/11/millennials-largest-generation-us-labor-force/.

71% of us would consider taking a pay cut to work for a company that has a mission they believe in and shared values.[145] It's why some big tech companies still have trouble recruiting younger top talent.[146]

Earlier this year, I let go of my nomadic ways when I decided to join Jambb for one simple reason: despite its size, *leadership* is already driving inclusive culture there. Every single person cares about the culture being inclusive, and they make it so. For everyone on the team, this team is home, and we're defining what success looks like together. The team is inclusive, and that is driving diversity, not the other way around. Three of their 10 or so team members identify as nonwhite women. There's a waitlist with women and other URGs interested in joining the team as the company receives more funding.

Our goal is to be representative of the Boston area, if not more so; Boston isn't super diverse.[147] About half of us are parents. There aren't meetings scheduled before work hours or after. The assumption is that people have their own lives that are just as crucial. Kids don't stop needing dinner just because you're busy being awesome. Remote work was already important to us pre-COVID-19, but now it's even more essential. This is what start-up life is like. We all work around each other, and Slack has become life. But when it's time for a sprint to a deadline, all the leaders are there too, showing up, telling people to go to bed. So as a tiny hat tip to people who have been supporting me throughout, let's talk about leading by example, like the team at Jambb is doing.

---

145 Nina McQueen, "Workplace Culture Trends: The Key to Hiring (and Keeping) Top Talent in 2018," *LinkedIn* (blog) (LinkedIn, June 26, 2018), https://blog. linkedin.com/2018/june/26/workplace-culture-trends-the-key-to-hiring-and-keeping-top-talent.

146 Millennials make up the generation that was born between 1980 and 1996; there seems to be some confusion on that.

147 Spotlight Team, "A Better Boston? The Choice Is Ours," *Boston Globe*, December 16, 2017, https://apps.bostonglobe.com/spotlight/boston-racism-image-reality/series/solutions/.

Leadership and Sponsorship

Since we're in chapter 10 of our relationship, I feel like I can tell you honestly: the only things you need to start acting out of allyship are the will to self-educate, the ability to recognize when you're wrong, and the willingness to fix it. Everything else we can teach. Now, you may be saying, "But where is the step-by-step guide to being an ally so I *never* mess up?!" There isn't one. Everyone messes up. Everyone is going to get it wrong from time to time, and that's what makes this journey hard, and why it requires leaders we can learn from.

More importantly, you have to be willing to learn in front of people. You have to be willing to learn to do hard things in front of people whose opinions matter to you. Recently, a friend who is an influencer and online community leader reached out to me. She was upset because a year prior, she had made choices informed by her ignorance of social justice issues, and now, people were calling her a racist. She was trying to mend fences by hosting a panel on Black Lives Matter and rolling out (some truly great) new initiatives that would be more inclusive and lead her followers in allyship and advocacy, but people were still calling her out.

"How can I do better if every time I open my mouth on this, people shout me down?" she lamented.

I had to answer honestly: "You might be doing the work now, but you aren't owning the impact you had when you didn't know better. You have to come out and admit that your ignorance clouded your judgment. You have to own that when women of color came to you to tell you that your followers were being racist and you didn't believe them, you were silencing Black voices. You have to own that your disbelief was rooted in ignorance and white supremacy. Fall on your sword with authenticity and humility, and ask your followers to help you rebuild and be more inclusive. It sounds awful, but people will rally around you if you are able to rebuild their trust the right way."

She disagreed with my advice for three days. Finally, she messaged me again: "Okay," she said, "I'm ready. Let's do it."

Some members of her community, who were clearly racist, asked her to stop bringing "politics" into her brand. Some people asked to have their money refunded, but the vast majority of members renewed their memberships and thanked her for her leadership on such a hard topic in such a difficult time. I'm not saying the same thing will work for everyone, but I am saying everyone needs to own their relationship with racism before they are able to move forward with any authenticity.

10 Principles for Inclusive Leadership

Why is there no how-to? Because these are interpersonal relationships, no two companies have the same inclusion issues. In fact, when I'm consulting, I'll sometimes see one team within the company is far more inclusive than other teams in the same company. That being understood, there are leadership principles that guide me based on interviews I've had and read from some of the top folks in our industry, and I'd like to share them with you.

1. If you want to build relationships with people, put your phone down, close your laptop, and *listen* to them. Especially in meetings. Focused attention on your coworkers builds trust and empathy.[148]

2. Build strong leaders by empowering and *educating* your managers. Development is crucial in businesses where they've seen so much growth that people have gone from individual contributors to managers in a very short amount of time.

---

148 Frances Frei and Anne Morriss, *Unleashed: The Unapologetic Leader's Guide to Empowering Everyone around You* (Boston, MA: Harvard Business Review Press, 2020).

Very few people will actually question whether or not they have the skills to lead people if they have already been promoted. Growth is a good thing, but we end up seeing titles outpacing individual abilities and unchecked biases filtering down into teams. You need to manage against this through development.

3. Create a decentralized model of decision-making authority; empower people to demonstrate good judgment from day one.

4. Use your hiring committees as hiring consultants, then make educated choices from there. A common practice when you have a diverse hiring committee is to allow someone to block a hire if absolutely necessary. For example, if two of your hiring committee members are really vibing with a candidate, but one of them is like, "Hey, this guy made a pass at me on the way in," it's probably not going to get more respectful from there. You need to have built enough trust to be able to take that advice no matter who it comes from.

5. If you have a brick-and-mortar office, build single-person, gender-inclusive bathrooms. Imagine if a nonbinary rock star candidate comes to your place of business. This person asks to use the bathroom in the middle of an all-day interview session, and neither of your binary bathrooms meets their needs. Are they going to join your team? Probably not.

6. Decide on your values. Write them down. Share them. Be transparent. These will be your anchoring tenets. One caveat: be neither too loose about them that you are blown over by public opinion, nor too rigid to adapt them if it's brought to your attention that these things aren't inclusive.

7. Build strong organizations that are flexible but scalable. Are you organized by function, or are you organized by business units? According to Claire Hughes Johnson, COO of Stripe, really

there are only these two. Check out the interview by Lattice on YouTube;[149] she's awesome.

8. Track your data. If you want to keep track of how you are doing with URGs, you need to be tracking your data through the entire employee life cycle. There are many companies that do this for you. If your only goal is to keep your numbers at a certain percentage, but in reality, your culture is so toxic that no one stays? Yes, 13% of your company is representing people of color, but if it's not the same people of color each year, what have you accomplished? Tokenism. Also, be sure to track the number of people you didn't hire for biases that you didn't notice you had.

9. Mentorship programs are great, but sponsorship programs are better. Incorporate sponsorship programs for members of your underrepresented groups. More on that below.

10. **Do the thing.** According to Jennifer Brown, "Change is about action. And if you aren't taking action, your silence is passive acceptance of the status quo, which further perpetuates the problem."[150]

Sponsorship over Mentorship

So you've rolled out a mentorship program that was a lot of work and a lot of time and money was invested, but you still aren't seeing the types of results you're looking for. What's going on here? Why are people touting mentorship programs if they don't work?

---

149 Claire Hughes Johnson: How Stripe's COO Approaches Company Building, interview by Jack Altman, *Lattice*, May 15, 2018, https://lattice.com/interview/coo-stripe.

150 Jennifer Brown, *How to Be an Inclusive Leader: Your Role in Creating Cultures of Belonging Where Everyone Can Thrive* (Oakland, CA: Berrett-Koehler Publishers, 2019).

What I'm noticing for the most part is confusion between terms and responsibilities. Mentorship programs do work to make employees feel more engaged, connected, and supported—they work for employee retention and satisfaction, but they don't always work when we measure how effective our mentorship programs have been for getting more URGs to the C-Suite. And with good reason. That's not the intention, or if it is the intention, what you're talking about is sponsorship.

Use Sponsorships to Promote DEI

Employees from underrepresented groups often enter the industry at a disadvantage because they may not have the same relationships and networks or common experiences as the rest of the team. Some companies attempt to level the playing field with mentors who offer tips and advice. However, their energies could be even better leveraged on a sponsorship program to connect employees with people in higher-ranking positions. Sponsors, unlike mentors, can provide opportunities in addition to guidance.

Becoming a successful sponsor isn't always a natural thing. Structure and a framework for sponsorship programs can help guide interactions and set expectations. Regular check-ins and a system for providing two-way feedback can also help. A successful sponsorship program should be clearly structured and voluntary for both parties, as the relationship requires trust and commitment. Also, if a sponsor–sponsee relationship isn't working, both parties should be able to withdraw without real or perceived penalties.

Setting clear goals to measure progress can also help increase the chances of a positive experience. Examples include targeting for a promotion within a set period of time, getting a raise, learning a new skill, leading a team project, or achieving another concrete career goal. Sponsors should be open about the kind of support they can provide to set a goal that they can help achieve.

People who are interested in sponsoring should be offered training to help them manage what could be a long-term collaborative relationship. Not everyone who would make a good sponsor will come forward, and your company should have a plan for identifying and reaching out to candidates. Their work should also be treated as the work that it is—this is not an add-on to existing projects, but a project in itself. Whether sponsors receive compensation, more time in their schedule, or other allowances, their contributions should be recognized. —Project Include[151]

Mentorship Responsibilities

A mentor is someone who is primarily a sounding board. They give good advice, help you make good decisions, and can guide and support you throughout your career. They often work at the same company as you, or usually in the same industry. Often, this is a person who shares your affinity and likes or cares about you. Mentors talk and you listen, but they aren't invested in your taking their advice. You have to rely on the goodness of others (and more importantly their time) as a mentee. But while all of those things are great and important for retention and satisfaction, how does this drive more diversity to the C-Suite and beyond?

Sylvia Ann Hewlett, CEO of Center of Talent Innovation, found that both men and women with sponsors are more likely to ask for high-profile assignments, pay raises, and promotions. Of the survey

---

151 "Employee Lifecycle," Project Include, accessed January 27, 2021, https://projectinclude.org/employee_lifecycle#use-sponsorships-to-promote-di. "Use sponsorships to promote DEI" subheading.

participants, 70% of men and 68% of women with sponsors felt more satisfied with their career advancement, compared to 57% of both men and women without sponsors. Even more encouraging is that minority employees with sponsors were 65% more satisfied than nonsponsored employees.

As she writes in her book *Forget a Mentor, Find a Sponsor*, "Mentors give, sponsors invest."

Sponsorship Responsibilities

A sponsor, by contrast, is someone who is invested in your success because it enhances or deepens their success. A sponsor, in addition to what a mentor would provide, helps you grow as a leader, covers you when you need to take risks, and advocates on your behalf for your next promotion. A sponsor fights for you when you aren't in the room and picks up the phone and makes those calls to promote you and your ambitions.

As Carla Harris, a Wall Street banker at Morgan Stanley, famously said: "All major decisions about your career will be made when you are not in the room."[152] This is why it is critical for people of underrepresented backgrounds to have sponsors. We are mentored at a much higher rate than white men, and we are sponsored at a much lower rate than white men, and in order to change anything, we need to spend our time and effort on what's having an impact. If you're only going to give me one, I want a sponsor. Sponsorship is how the Good Ol' Boys[153] network has flourished in the past (and still does).

---

152 Hilary Burns, "4 'Pearls of Wisdom' on How to Succeed from a Wall Street Banker," The Business Journals, November 11, 2014, https://www.bizjournals. com/bizjournals/how-to/growth-strategies/2014/11/carla-harris-morgan-stanley-pearls-of-wisdom.html

153 A Good Ol' Boys network is when leaders hire, promote, and sponsor subordinates who are their favorites. Usually favorites who look like them. They may have gone to the same (elite) schools or belong to the same groups and communities. Nepotism is another variation of this as it is also not merit based.

I'm a Black woman, and my parents are immigrants; they worked hard to make sure I was in the best schools in Brooklyn, from grammar school up through college. When I worked for this one company, I'd already had years of advertising experience under my belt. I worked there for three years. I started on social media, and by the time I was leaving, I had run several good campaigns for the company that helped them grow quite a bit. My team was doing well, everything was awesome.

But they decided to hire a friend of a guy who is a close personal friend to Jack Dorsey [CEO of Twitter and others], and they put him over me in the hierarchy. He was a "bro" type of guy who had no experience in what he was doing. He wanted to micromanage me, he wanted to micromanage my team, and every time something went wrong, even things that didn't matter, he would publicly shame and berate me, often citing my race or my gender as why "his projects" were unsuccessful. Which they weren't. He would slam me on Slack, tagging his boss, and he would write lengthy, awful emails about me and copy everyone he could think of.

No one stuck up for me, no one said anything because they didn't want their careers to be over, and this guy was petty. Once when I was running a photo shoot, I noticed a mistake he had made, I brought it to his attention, just to let him know we'd have to fix it, and he went ballistic. I fixed the mistake anyway, and the project went off with no further issues. He worked hard to blame me for it and then took credit for the save.

I ran into a friend of his after the photo shoot and after I decided to spend my talent on someone who respected me and wasn't an obvious misogynist, and the friend told me I should visit the guy the next time I was in town because I was his favorite employee. Um, no thanks. Maybe he liked telling people I was his favorite employee, maybe it bought him credibility as anything other than what he was, but I left there and I'll never be back.

—D.K., credit card processing company

When I talk about sponsorship over mentorship, I am arguing, as Sylvia Ann Hewlett has, that sponsorship has a measurable positive impact on the careers of URGs.

Furthermore, sponsorship as a rule is a win-win and a largely transactional relationship. You sponsor me because you believe I'm good for your brand. I will loyally defend you. I will cover your blind side, and I will make sure that people beneath you and around you aren't sowing the seeds of disloyalty or trying to oust you. I will make sure you don't look stupid when you make comments about social issues. In turn, you make sure that when the door is closed and I'm on the other side of it, that people are treating me fairly, and that I'm getting ahead when I deserve it. You make phone calls on my behalf because you know I'm out here doing the same for you. My sponsors need me because they know they can call anytime with an issue that could get hot and public fast, and I can advise them how to positively affect hard situations. I deepen their bench, and C-Suite occupants need that more than ever.

According to Sara Berhané in *Fast Company*: "There are plenty of mentoring programs out there these days for professional women, but they aren't doing enough. Many are held up as examples of a company's commitment to diversifying its leadership pipeline, but despite the resources and good intentions behind such programs, they rarely bring about real change. Few of the employees who participate tend to advance as far as they could, and the corporation's glass ceiling stays intact. And it's much the same in less-formal mentoring contexts, too."[154]

---

154 Sava Berhané, "Why Women Need Career Sponsors More than Mentors," *Fast Company*, August 28, 2015, https://www.fastcompany.com/3050430/why-women-need-career-sponsors-more-than-mentors.

Hugh Welsh of DSM adds: "My personal experience shows intentional sponsorship can drive the required change in recruiting, retaining, developing, and deploying talent regardless of race, gender, or ethnicity that every organization aspires to achieve. In the past few years at DSM, I've taken on four promising employees as my own experiment testing this theory. All were diverse by age, gender, and ethnicity; and none of them were among the organization's leadership at the time. They did share one trait: I believed they were among the most talented people in our company. The results: all four were promoted; all four moved across different businesses in DSM, a key development goal; and three have already been promoted to the executive ranks in DSM."[155] He goes on to share that each of these protégés has become leadership at DSM, and he has taken on new protégés as a result, as they have. He says that since DSM already ties executive compensation to sustainability, adding intentional sponsorship programs to executive compensation wasn't a big leap.

Now, I've heard the arguments against sponsorship:

"I don't want managers coming in and arguing for people who don't deserve it in my meetings. We have a flat organization!"

Okay. No, you don't. Unless your CEO and your engineers and your office manager make the same amount, you don't have a flat organization. You still have a hierarchy, just instead of traditional "organizational politics," you have one based on compensation. Comp is one of the ways we show people how much we value their work. Obviously. While in a flat org, you are removing layers that can hold back innovation, you might also notice you have more inclusion issues. Again, pretending systems of inequality don't exist doesn't make it easier for people not in positions of power. It just lays the blame for

---

155 Hugh Welsh, "Sponsorship Has More Promise for Executive Diversity than Mentorship," *Entrepreneur*, May 27, 2016, https://www.entrepreneur.com/article/274525.

inequality at their door and removes any power and opportunity for us to correct it.

"Why are we engaging in the Good Ol' Boys network? Why don't we just not do that"?

Look, I'm not arguing *for* the Good Ol' Boys network or any elitist system that drives people to the top of an organization without merit. I didn't set this system up. It has existed well before me and will exist long after me. As everyone who isn't in a position of power knows well, this world is already unfair, companies aren't always equal, and we aren't going to see that go away. We aren't going to get ahead by continuing to pretend business is a meritocracy. It isn't. So what can we do instead? We can expand our access to these networks by acknowledging them, studying them, and making them work for us all.

Leading up the Mountain

When talking to more privileged groups about oppressive systems in the workplace, I am often met with an entirely uphill battle. On the one hand, yes, people of color and other marginalized groups do want me there discussing and facilitating solutions to the challenges I'm seeing in their workplace, but they are skeptical. Firstly, will I say anything real; and secondly, will anything I say have an impact on their workplaces? You as a leader may be seeing the same uphill battle. People in privileged positions are going to fight you and say nothing is wrong, and people in marginalized positions are going to view your efforts with distrust. So why bother?

Because an injustice for anyone is an injustice for everyone. If any person in your workplace has to cover at work, it is likely that everyone is covering at work to some degree. Whether it's a mother who isn't talking about her children so she seems committed to the job or someone who appears to be a white man awkwardly avoiding pronouns when he talks about his partner, or a Latinx millennial who doesn't come to after-hours events because they have to care for an ailing parent, or a Muslim employee who doesn't drink and doesn't want you to know why because of stereotype threat[156]—these are just some of the obvious ways people cover at work. And covering at work leads to people leaving some of their best selves behind, and their best selves are where all their good ideas and diverse perspectives are. They aren't coming with them in a place where everyone strives to meet the white, male standard known as "professionalism."

When I interviewed Tony Awojoodu, PhD and Founder and CEO of Tone's Professional Advisory Solutions & Services, we chatted about his experience with "professional" standards. "Coming up in DC, we had diverse classrooms: Black teachers, Black leaders, Black causes, and organizations," he said. "But when I joined McKinsey, after graduate school, it was really the first time I felt different because of my skin. I would walk into a room and be the only Black person at the table helping the company leaders make decisions that would have enormous impact. It made me hyperconscious of my Blackness. I shaved my head and my face and tried to overcompensate to fit in with these coworkers, who were as smart and as talented as me, but they were largely white or Indian. I felt like if I failed, it wasn't just myself I was failing. I was failing all the Black folks that would come after me. That has an impact. That does harm."

So what's the easiest way to have this conversation in teams? Reframe the conversation. Everyone has a diversity story. Everyone has something that makes them a little different that is needed on your teams and is shared by your consumers. While in this line of work, it's crucial that we celebrate and support people of marginalized identities (rightly), and sometimes that can make white folks and white males in particular feel like they don't have a part to play—and that causes some

---

156 All true examples from interviews.

defensiveness. Instead, I recommend you give them a role: fighting ally and advocate. Lily Zheng, writing for *Harvard Business Review*, poses the following: "Consider this statement: 'White people have a powerful and partial understanding of how race works in society.' Statements like these name a privileged identity (white), attach constrained value to it (powerful and partial), and then situate it in a context that encourages future conversation (how race works in society). They are also easy to expand into larger conversations with questions like, 'How do other racial groups understand how race works in society? How are their experiences different? Why?'"[157]

TL;DR:

- Spotting the diamond in the rough when it comes to talent is a skill you will need to develop, especially if you are a start-up and want to win the war for talent. Building a strong and inclusive culture will attract members of URGs and help you build a more diverse and talented pipeline.

- Millennials are 50% of the workforce, and we care more about the company's values than compensation.

- There is no leadership "how-to" for never messing up on issues of diversity and inclusion. You can fail with authenticity and model how to do better and still be considered an awesome leader.

- Put your phone down during meetings. It helps build psychological safety and trust.

- Use your hiring committee as hiring consultants, and make informed decisions on hiring. Stop hiring from your network.

---

157 Lily Zheng, "How to Show White Men That Diversity and Inclusion Efforts Need Them," *Harvard Business Review*, October 28, 2019, https://hbr. org/2019/10/how-to-show-white-men-that-diversity-and-inclusion-efforts-need-them.h

- Sponsorship > Mentorship.
- "Professionalism" is a white, male standard. The closer you are to it, the more qualified you'll be considered with less experience. You also get idiosyncrasy credits, allowing you to wear the same outfit every day and having people think that's genius vs. crazy. Black women, on the other hand, can expect to have fewer job offers if they wear their hair naturally.[158] Think about how those "standards" impact your workforce.

---

158 Jack Guy, "Black Women with Natural Hairstyles Are Less Likely to Get Job Interviews," CNN, August 12, 2020, https://www.cnn.com/2020/08/12/business/black-women-hairstyles-interview-scli-intl-scn/index.html.

CONCLUSION

"We don't climb the mountain so we can look down on everyone else. We climb the mountain so we can turn around and pull others up with us."

—Alex Toussaint

This might be what you're thinking right now: "So, Di, I've accepted that what you've been telling me is true. I can see that my team is largely white, and that that means I haven't been focusing on inclusion and bringing more people in. In fact, our entire industry is largely white. I've moved past the 'self-flagellation' stage into the action stage. When I discussed this with my team and asked for their ideas, I received a lot of pushback about how this wasn't my problem to solve and that I was 'acting like a white knight,' and it wasn't my place to have an opinion on this or focus our efforts on this. How do you, a white woman, deal with that criticism both on your team and from strangers? How do I have any opinion at all as a white person?"

I'm always glad when this question comes up, and I want to address it here because if there is only one thing that you take away from this book, let it be this: systemic racism is something white folks benefit

153

from, and until it is seen as a white issue to solve and not just an issue for "woke" white folks to empathize with, nothing will ever change. Inequality is your responsibility. You have skin in the game. You have to do the work to solve this problem in the workplace. It needs to be seen as a problem for your company, and we need to solve it the way we would solve any other business issue.

Allow me to show you what I mean: let's say you have a race condition,[159] and something is loading before everything else in its sequence. It can be really hard to track down and debug because you don't know where it starts. It basically lives in infamy, right? Okay. So what would you do? You'd assign tickets, you'd assign resources, and you'd deal with it until you worked out the root of your issue to make changes. And if what you thought was the problem wasn't the problem, would you give up or keep iterating? You'd keep iterating. That is how you deal with any issue in business except inequality. Because we'd rather not see inequality, we have a tendency to ignore it or put a bandage on a bullet wound and think, "We'll get to this later," or worse, "This isn't my problem to solve." It's everyone's problem to solve. Everyone has a diversity story.

To be sure, we want to make sure that we are not acting as "white saviors." White folks should not walk into a space and think no work has been happening before they got there. For example, "I am here now to save you all, people of color or women+ or nonbinary employees or LGBTQ+ employees!" That is being a white savior or a white knight. Don't do that.

Instead, what you should do is self-educate to the best of your ability. *Read*. Assign resources. Work with (and learn from) your people. You are joining a resistance already in progress, so become part of the existing fabric. Take classes on allyship. I literally teach them.[160] Demonstrate

---

159 I know; life is ironic.
160 Join one at www.diciruolo.com.

your willingness to learn *in public*, and model that authenticity for your employees and coworkers. Always be learning. You will not always be right, but failing forward will help others follow you.

I did everything I could to avoid writing this book. It's weird to say, but it's a hard and emotionally charged topic—there was going to be a blowback no matter how hard I worked to get it right. I expected personal attacks and criticism about myself or my experience. So I wanted someone with a more perfect background, a more perfect pedigree, someone who was different than me to write it. After waiting and praying and avoiding, it finally occurred to me through everyone I spoke with: if I was too scared to demonstrate doing advocacy work in public, in the arena, with the trolls and the haters, and people who would tell me I was too white or too uneducated or too privileged, then I had no right to ask anyone else to.

I started writing in 2019, and in January of 2020, Google was (not so) quietly scaling back their diversity and inclusion team.[161] People sent me articles that declared "Diversity's time in the sun was over." Google now denies this. An executive who had previously wanted to work with me laughed in my face and suggested I "find a new hustle." But I didn't quit because I know this work matters. This is a lifelong effort, even if I'm the only one who shows up.

"To escape criticism, do nothing, say nothing, be nothing."
—Elbert Hubbard.

For my part, I am not special. I do not have a degree in every culture, language, and history. I do have a degree in this field, but as I say, there

---

161 April Glaser, "Current and Ex-Employees Allege Google Drastically Rolled Back Diversity Programs," NBC News, May 13, 2020, https://www.nbcnews. com/news/us-news/current-ex-employees-allege-google-drastically-rolled-back-diversity-inclusion-n1206181.

are definitely folks more educated than I am. I wasn't born into the upper or even middle class. I was born into absolute poverty. We were on food stamps. The edges of society. The woman who gave birth to me is still living in public housing to this day. We still don't talk. I've been homeless. I've been so poor I couldn't eat. I know what you can get off the dollar menu at McDonald's and survive. I know about the choice between rent and your car. I know about group homes. I know about being put on medication you don't need in foster care. I know about the foster-care-to-prison pipeline. I have survivor's guilt. I know about staying in abusive relationships so you aren't homeless. I'm here anyway. I graduated from a good college anyway. I don't know a single person like me. Maybe I need to be the person I always needed.

My point in saying all this is if I can do this, if I can find a way to fight for equality, you have to find a way to make your stand too. You don't have to wait for permission. You don't have to wait until everything else is perfect. You can get started while you're in progress, like me. You don't have to change everything all at once; you can change one thing every day, every week, every month and still be in the fight for equality. But don't go slowly out of fear of messing up. And never fake it.

This book, this work, is my stand. When our children look back at us in this moment and say, "What did you do when you knew things were wrong and you had the power to change it?" Consider how that conversation will go, and be who you want them to be. I have. Build the world you want them to live in. I am. Don't be that person who wants everyone to have it hard because they have had it hard. Build bridges and longer tables, not walls and VIP lists. If I can do it, you can.

ACKNOWLEDGMENTS

To say that I stand on the shoulders of giants would be a huge understatement here; so please believe me when I say this book would not have been possible without the writers, the thinkers, the activists, and the women+ of color who have done and will continue to do the work in my field. Beyond crediting every author in the footnotes, I would like to credit every single one of the hundreds of interviewees who trusted me enough to share their story and push me toward authenticity in my voice and my research. I would like to thank the editing team and writing coaches that worked with me on this enormous undertaking: Nick for believing in the subject matter and organizing my thoughts; Sarah, Jennifer, and Catherine for keeping them coherent; and Keri for driving me to always reach higher.

To Bert Weiss and Tyler Perry, y'all changed my life just by sharing your authentic story and nudged me back into my lane. No words can express my gratitude for your grace.

I would like to thank my incredible publishing team at Morgan James for all of their input and support. Because I don't have a traditional family, I've been adopted by and have adopted many members of my family of creation. I would like to thank every single one of you for taking my anxiety-riddled texts, hooking me up with leaders, and believing in me and my abilities regardless of my humble beginnings. Thank you, fam.

Lastly, there have been a lot of people throughout my life who have told me I couldn't do something because of where I came from, and to those folks I say: I probably would not have made it this far if I didn't have the drive to prove you wrong. So, thank you.

SOCIAL JUSTICE RESOURCES:

The root of any DEI work is social justice, and I stand on the shoulders of giants. We all do. Here are some resources that will help build your knowledge and vocabulary.[162]

Race, Privilege & Bias:

- *How to Be an Antiracist* by Ibram X. Kendi
- *So You Want to Talk about Race* by Ijeoma Oluo
- *White Rage* by Carol Anderson
- *White Fragility* by Robin DiAngelo
- *Me and White Supremacy* by Layla F. Saad
- *Between the World and Me* by Ta-Nehisi Coates
- *The Fire Next Time* by James Baldwin
- *Why Are All the Black Kids Sitting Together in the Cafeteria?* by Beverly Daniel Tatum
- *Sister Outsider* by Audre Lorde
- *Fatal Invention* by Dorothy E. Roberts

---

162 In no order, just as I grabbed them around my workspace—my books are a design choice at this point.

- *The Color of Water: A Black Man's Tribute to His White Mother* by James McBride
- *Beloved* by Toni Morrison
- *Heavy: An American Memoir* by Kiese Laymon
- *The Hate U Give* by Angie Thomas
- *I'm Still Here: Black Dignity in a World Made for Whiteness* by Austin Channing Brown
- *We Should All be Feminists* by Chimamanda Ngozi Adichie
- *Belonging* by bell hooks
- *No, You Shut Up* by Symone D. Sanders[163]
- *Gender Ambiguity in The Workplace* by Alison Ash Fogarty and Lily Zheng
- *Belonging at Work* by Rhodes Perry
- *The Memo* by Minda Harts

History:
- *Stamped from the Beginning* by Ibram X. Kendi
- *Homegoing* by Yaa Gyasi
- *The Color of Law* by Richard Rothstein
- *The Half Has Never Been Told: Slavery and the Making of American Capitalism* by Edward E. Baptist
- *An African American and Latinx History of the United States* by Paul Ortiz
- *The Autobiography of Malcolm X. as told to Alex Haley*
- *The New Jim Crow* by Michelle Alexander
- *The 1619 Project*[164]
- *The Souls of Black Folk* by W. E. B. DuBois

---

163 I met Symone at a women's+ event, and she is everything.
164 Jake Silverstein, "Why We Published the 1619 Project," *New York Times Magazine*, December 20, 2019, https://www.nytimes.com/interactive/2019/12/20/magazine/1619-intro.html.

- *Letters from the Birmingham Jail* by Martin Luther King, Jr.
- *The Warmth of Other Suns* by Isabel Wilkerson
- *March* by John Lewis[165] et. al (an awesome three-part graphic novel)

Watch:

- *Uncomfortable Conversations with a Black Man* with Emmanuel Acho (via Instagram)
- *The Great Unlearn* with Rachel Cargle
- *Selma* (2014)
- *I Am Not Your Negro* (2016)
- *The Hate U Give* (2018)
- *Let It Fall: Los Angeles 1982–1992* (2017)
- *13th* (2016) by Ava DuVernay[166]
- *Just Mercy* (2019)
- *Fruitvale Station* (2013)
- *Time: The Kalief Browder Story* (2017)
- *Teach Us All* (2017)
- *Flint Town* (2018)
- *Emanuel* (2019)
- *Loving* (2016)
- *The Oprah Conversation* (2020, Apple TV)
- *Roots* (1977 and/or 2016)
- *12 Years a Slave* (2013) based on the book of the same name by Solomon Northup
- *Harriet* (2019)

---

165 In my time in Atlanta, I was able to meet John Lewis twice and hear him speak. He was absolutely the best of us.
166 Follow all her film work. Forever.

Medium:

- Marley K
- Carl Anka
- Sage Lazzaro
- Dr. Tracey A. Benson
- The Only Black Guy in the Office
- Ezinne Ukoha
- S. Rae Peoples
- Kym Motley
- Ruth Terry
- Naomi Day
- Ajah Hales
- Amina Adewusi
- Seanna Wong
- Dr. David Campt
- Michelle Kim
- Stanley Fritz

Podcasts:

- *Code Switch* (NPR)
- *Still Processing*
- *We Are Meaningful*
- *The Daily*
- *1619*
- *Pod Save the People*
- *Yo, Is This Racist?*
- *Seeing White*
- *Mixed Company*
- *#Techish*
- *The Nod*
- *Momentum*

- *Higher Learning*
- *The United States of Anxiety*
- *74 Seconds*
- *Come Through*
- *The Stoop*
- *Groundings*
- *The Will to Change*
- Y'all Hiring?

Anti-Racist Children's Books:
- *Antiracist Baby* by Ibram X. Kendi
- *Let the Children March* by Monica Clark-Robinson
- *Something Happened in Our Town* by Marianne Celano, Marietta Collins, and Ann Hazzard
- *The Day You Begin* by Jacqueline Woodson
- *Little Leaders Series: Bold Women in Black History* by Vashti Harrison
- *Voice of Freedom* by Carole Boston Weatherford
- *Bedtime Inspirational Stories* by L.A. Amber
- *Sit-In* by Andrea Davis Pinkney
- *Heart and Soul* by Kadir Nelson
- *A Children's Introduction to African American History* by Jabari Asim

Follow:[167]
- @emmanuelacho (IG)
- @BreeNewsome (TW)
- @IjeomaOluo (FB, TW)
- @austinchanning (FB, TW)

---

167 Again, not remotely exhaustive. Not even everyone I follow, but a good starting point to be shown other influencers and leaders.

- @accordingtoweeze (IG)
- @gabestorres (IG)
- Michelle Kim (LI)
- @sincerely.lettie (IG)
- Jennifer Brown (LI)
- @_dyanedwards (IG)
- @blackcoffeewithwhitefriends (IG)
- @iamderay (IG)
- @coolurbanhippie (IG)
- @blackfemaletherapists (IG)
- @ebonyjanice (IG)
- @ibramxk (IG)
- Lily Zheng (LI)
- Aubrey Blanche (LI)
- Jenny Wong (LI)
- @bethebridge (IG)
- @ethelsclub (IG)
- @equalitylabs (IG)
- Tara Jaye Frank (LI)
- Roz Francuz-Harris (LI)
- Jodi-Ann Burey (LI)
- Rhodes Perry (LI)
- @mskellymhayes (TW)
- @rachel.cargle (IG)
- @strongblacklead (IG)
- @survivepunish (TW)
- @amandaseales (IG)
- @cthagod (IG)
- @hood_biologist (TW, IG)
- @black_womenlead (IG)
- @mysonnenygeneral (IG)

- @symonedsanders (IG)
- Crystal Johnson (LI)
- Brittany J. Harris (LI)
- Madison Butler (LI)

ABOUT THE AUTHOR

 Dianna Machado Ciruolo has a degree in anthropology from Georgia State University. She is a white-Hispanic, queer woman living in Boston, Massachusetts, where she graduated from the foster care system as a young adult. She now owns a consulting business teaching inclusion and advocacy in the workplace, with classes available at diciruolo.com. She is the Head of Inclusion at Jambb in Boston. She has written articles for Medium and is an obsessive reader. She volunteers on several inclusion projects especially expanding access to tech education for children in foster care. She is a space-maker and semi reluctant public speaker. She is married to her partner, Jay, and they have two fiery children.

A free ebook edition is available with the purchase of this book.

To claim your free ebook edition:

Visit MorganJamesBOGO.com
Sign your name CLEARLY in the space
Complete the form and submit a photo of
the entire copyright page
You or your friend can download the ebook
to your preferred device

Morgan James
BOGO™

A **FREE** ebook edition is available for you
or a friend with the purchase of this print book.

CLEARLY SIGN YOUR NAME ABOVE

Instructions to claim your free ebook edition:
1. Visit MorganJamesBOGO.com
2. Sign your name CLEARLY in the space above
3. Complete the form and submit a photo
   of this entire page
4. You or your friend can download the ebook
   to your preferred device

Print & Digital Together Forever.

Snap a photo

Free ebook

Read anywhere

Printed in the USA
CPSIA information can be obtained
at www.ICGtesting.com
JSHW022331140824
68134JS00019B/1417